South Dakota

SOUTH DAKOTA BY ROAD

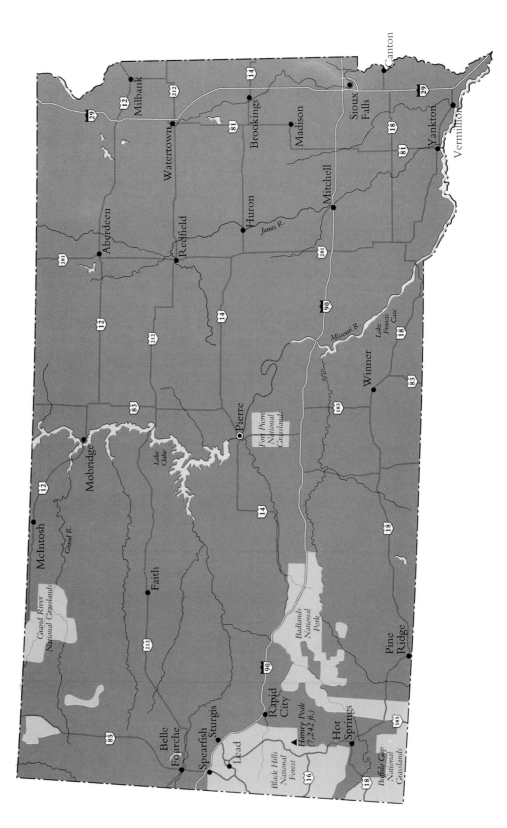

Celebrate the States

South Dakota

Melissa McDaniel

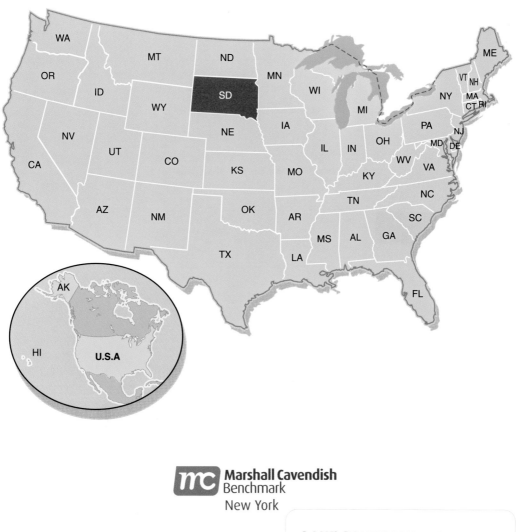

mc Marshall Cavendish
Benchmark
New York

Marshall Cavendish Benchmark
99 White Plains Road
Tarrytown, NY 10591-9001
www.marshallcavendish.us

Library of Congress Cataloging-in-Publication Data
McDaniel, Melissa, 1964–
South Dakota / by Melissa McDaniel.—2nd ed.
p. cm. — (Celebrate the states)
Summary: "Provides comprehensive information on the geography, history, wildlife, governmental
structure, economy, cultural diversity, peoples, religion, and landmarks of South Dakota"—Provided
by publisher.
Includes bibliographical references and index.
ISBN-13: 978-0-7614-2156-6
ISBN-10: 0-7614-2156-4
South Dakota—Juvenile literature. I. Title. II. Series.
F651.3.M33 2006
978.3—dc22   2005027083

Editor: Christine Florie
Editorial Director: Michelle Bisson
Art Director: Anahid Hamparian
Series Designer: Adam Mietlowski

Photo Research by Candlepants Incorporated

Cover Photo: Dallas & John Heaton/Corbis

The photographs in this book are used by permission and through the courtesy of; *Corbis:* David
Muench, 8, 100; Tom Bean, 10, 20; Corbis, 11, 31, 36,47, 95, 126, 130; Pat O'Hara, 15; Richard T.
Nowitz, 17; Jeff Vanuga, 27; Bettmann, 33, 34, 37, 39,48, 123, 127,129; John C. H. Grabill, 38; W.R.
Cross, 43; Annie Griffiths Belt, 50; Jan Butchofsky-Houser, 53; Ed Kashi, 56, 57; Allen Smith, 72;
Charles Rotkin, 74; Russ Munn, 76; Dave Bartruff, 79, 84; Kevin Fleming, 83; Layne Kennedy, 103,
108; George H.H. Huey, 105(top); Theo Allofs, 105(bottom); D. Robert & Lorri Franz, 109; Joseph
Sohm, 113; David Turnley, 119; Underwood & Underwood, 120; Owen Franklin, 121; Gregory Pace,
124; Wally McNamee,125; Nik Wheeler, 133; Paul Souders, 134; Joseph Sohm/Chromosohm Inc., 137.
Minden Pictures: Jim Brandenburg, 16, 19, 21. *South Dakota Dept. of Tourism:* 18, 59, 64, 89, 91, 92,
97, 98, 115, 117, 131. *AP/Wide World Photos:* Val Hoeppner, 23; J. Scott Park, 32; Doug Dryer, 25, 66,
69; Bob Jordan, 80. *Bridgeman Art Library:* Private Collection, The Stapleton Collection, 28; Private
Collection, Peter Newark Western Americana, 30. *Index Stock:* Allen Russell, 61, 82; Todd Powell, 101.
The Image Works: Andre Jenny, 68, 86, 87; Ralph Neimzig, 99.

Printed in China
1 3 5 6 4 2

Contents

South Dakota Is . . .

South Dakota is peaceful . . .

"[T]here's just something about the plains. Out here, you can really see the stars."

—Joanne Harmon, Sturgis resident

"I like it. When you go outside and you can see for a million miles, you can think a little bit."

—Twelve-year-old South Dakotan

. . . and it is quiet.

"There was something else here. . . . It was an enormous stillness that made you feel still. And when you were still, you could feel great stillness coming closer. All the little sounds of the blowing grasses and of the horses munching . . . and even the sounds of eating and talking could not touch the enormous silence of the prairie."

—Laura Ingalls Wilder, novelist

It is home to hard workers.

"My father no longer wrestles a team of horses and a clumsy wagon to haul dirt. . . . Still, he works hard. . . . Hard work is a legacy of the generations who settled the prairie, broke the soil, built the sod houses, fought the droughts and grasshoppers and penny-a-pound prices for their products."

—Tom Brokaw, television journalist born and raised in Webster

And it is a place where people live at a slower pace.

"On the plains . . . we also treasure our world-champion slow talkers, people who speak as if God has given them only so many words to use in a lifetime, and having said them they will die."

—Kathleen Norris, South Dakota writer

Not everyone appreciates South Dakota . . .

"A friend of mine asked what . . . our ancestors were thinking, settling here. We have the coldest cold and the hottest hot. But the last time we had to lock our cars around here was for no reason."

—Neil Brakke, Presho resident

. . . but some people would not want to live anywhere else.

"There. Right there, where the land begins to flatten out and the trees disappear. That's where I want to live."

—Dan O'Brien, writer and buffalo rancher

South Dakota is a state of magnificent landscapes. It has striking mountains, eerie badlands, and rolling plains. It is home to friendly farmers, resilient Native Americans, and fierce individualists—the sons and daughters of pioneers, warriors, cowboys, miners, and anyone else who wanted plenty of space between them and the next person. It is a state where history was not such a long time ago, so its echoes linger still.

Chapter One

Prairie and Beyond

Not many people live in South Dakota. With just over 770,000 residents, it's the fifth-smallest state by population. But a lot of people who have never been to South Dakota think they know what it's like. Ask anyone and they'll tell you: it's flat. They're right—and wrong.

The Missouri River runs south through the middle of South Dakota, splitting the state into two roughly equal parts known as East River and West River. East River has more fertile land and a larger population. This is the part that is flat. West River has drier land that is more suitable to grazing than to farming; it also boasts the most notable geographic features in the state—the Black Hills and the Badlands.

EAST RIVER

When people say South Dakota is flat, they are generally talking about East River. But even here it is not entirely true. Ask any bicyclist. After pedaling across the state, journalist Bruce Weber concluded, "It's a myth, by the

A vast majority of the Pine Ridge Indian Reservation is wild prairie.

A road peaks and dips through the Grand River National Grassland.

way, that South Dakota is flat. The prairie is an undulating one . . . with the road making great dips and swirls that are visible for miles in either direction. Bicycling through this is hard."

The southern part of East River country is the best agricultural land in the state, a land of gentle, rolling prairies. It is home to most of South Dakota's farms, as well as most of its people.

Farther north, the hills, while still low, are more apparent. Often nestled among them are lakes and small ponds called prairie potholes. Some of these watering holes exist only in the spring, after the thaw and before the parched summer. Others disappear only in times of drought.

A group of buffalo graze around a prairie pothole in Custer State Park.

They are all important to the state's animals—not to mention its people, since many make excellent swimming holes.

Moving west toward the Missouri River, the land becomes drier, the landscape browner, and the ponds fewer. Towns are farther apart. Most of this country is too dry for crops to grow. Instead, cattle and sheep graze on the scrubby grass.

WEST RIVER

West River is even less hospitable to agricultural activities. Just west of the Missouri, the hills become steeper and closer together. They rise one after another in strange, twisted shapes. The northwestern part of the state is flatter, except for its many huge buttes (isolated hills or mountains with steep sides and a flat top) that loom over the plains. Some of these buttes are as much as six hundred feet tall. West River gets less rain than East River, so the land is often beige in color. That suits West River people just fine. "May and June are too green," says Spearfish resident Paul Higbee. He prefers that "West River, semiarid brown" because he doesn't have to worry about mowing the lawn.

This desolate land provides few ways to make a living. With the exception of the Black Hills, West River is very sparsely inhabited, averaging only about five people per square mile. The population bottoms out in Harding County, in the state's northwest corner, which has less than one person per square mile. In the nineteenth century, when white settlers were still spreading over the continent, the definition of frontier was "having fewer than two people per square mile." Eleven of South Dakota's sixty-six counties still fit that definition.

LAND AND WATER

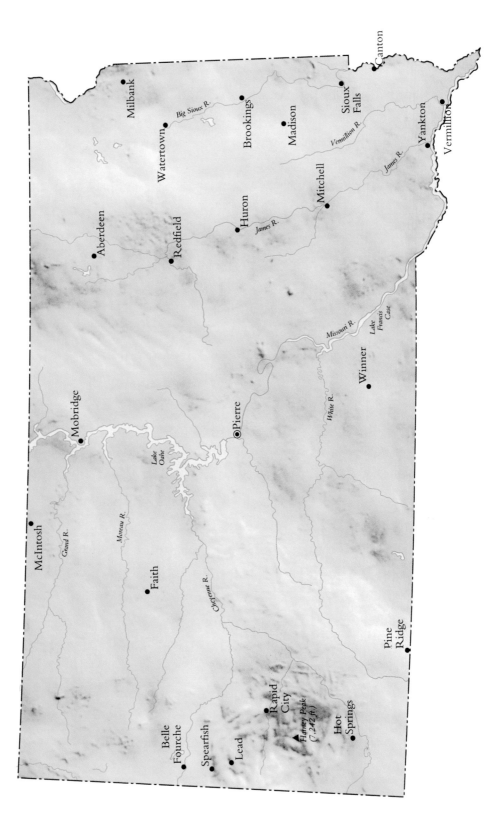

Canton

Milbank

Big Sioux R.

Brookings

Sioux Falls

Madison

Vermillion R.

Yankton

Vermillion

Watertown

Mitchell

James R.

Aberdeen

Redfield

Huron

James R.

Lake Francis Case

Missouri R.

Winner

Mobridge

White R.

Lake Oahe

Pierre

McIntosh

Grand R.

Moreau R.

Faith

Cheyenne R.

Pine Ridge

Belle Fourche

Spearfish

Lead

Rapid City

Harney Peak (7,242 ft.)

Hot Springs

BADLANDS AND BLACK HILLS

The Badlands rise out of the prairie in the southwest part of the state. They are one of the most unusual and remarkable landforms in the United States. This rugged, desolate region is marked by craggy ravines, eroded cliffs, and peculiar spires.

When the famous American architect Frank Lloyd Wright first saw the Badlands in 1935, he had already been all over the world, but nothing had prepared him for the sight. He wrote to a friend: "ethereal in color and exquisitely chiseled in endless detail, [the Badlands] began to reach to infinity spreading into the sky on every side; an endless supernatural world more spiritual than earth but created out of it."

There are many badlands in the United States. The word is used for any area where water erosion has worn away soft rock and left narrow canyons and drainage creeks that are dry most of the year. In South Dakota, though, the effect is particularly mesmerizing because minerals have left stripes of different colors in the soil.

These colors are the result of South Dakota's geologic history. Seventy million years ago there was vast ocean over the Great Plains. By about 65 million years ago it had disappeared, leaving a bed of black shale on which a jungle sprang up. Then tree roots broke up the shale, and dead plant material rotted away, turning the shale into a bright yellow soil. Succeeding eras of jungle and forest and flood added new layers and colors.

About a half-million years ago, wind and water began to erode the soil, exposing its different colors. This erosion has never stopped, and it is still creating a slowly changing landscape. The erosion continually unearths new fossils: remnants of clams and oysters that lived in the inland ocean and of great tree roots that grew beside streams in lush forests—all evidence of the millions of years that went into producing the Badlands.

In the Badlands, each distinctly colored layer of rock represents a different time in Earth's history.

Although the Badlands look barren, they actually support abundant life. Rabbits, snakes, prairie dogs, meadowlarks, curlews, eagles, and even buffalo live among their shadows. Badlands National Park is home to about fifty kinds of grasses and more than four hundred types of plants. A single pink blossom clinging to the side of a craggy cliff is somehow more beautiful in its isolation. Juniper, yucca, wild rose, sumac, and other plants grow in the Badlands wherever the slightest bit of water is found.

The only prairie dog species living in South Dakota is the black-tailed prairie dog. Over 200,000 prairie dogs live in the state.

During the summer, the Badlands come to life with blooming wildflowers.

To the west are the Black Hills, the other outstanding landform in South Dakota. The hills were named by the Lakota Sioux, who called them *Paha Sapa,* or "Hills of Black." From afar, the slopes appear black, because they are covered with dark pines. South Dakota's highest spot, Harney Peak, is in the Black Hills. It reaches 7,242 feet high and is also the highest point in the United States east of the Rocky Mountains. The beauty of the Black Hills is legendary. They are renowned for their towering granite spires and magnificent canyons. In the lush forests of ponderosa pine, spruce, and aspen, many people enjoy walking on beds of pine needles, past gurgling creeks and stony outcroppings.

A sacred area to the Sioux, and later highly valued by early gold-seeking pioneers, the Black Hills offer unparalleled scenery and wildlife.

In 1803 the young United States bought the Louisiana Territory from France. This vast territory stretched from the Mississippi River to the Rocky Mountains, from New Orleans to Canada. The following year Meriwether Lewis and William Clark headed an expedition to map the new territory and gather information about its plant and animal life, natural formations, and native inhabitants. Traveling up the Missouri River through what is now South Dakota, Lewis and Clark were overwhelmed by the immense quantity and variety of wildlife, the great herds of pronghorns, elks, and bison. Although South Dakota no longer has the natural abundance it did then, it still supports a wonderful array of wildlife, particularly in the Black Hills. The state is home to white-tailed deer, mule deer, pronghorns, elks, bighorn sheep, coyotes, prairie dogs, beavers, rattlesnakes, muskrats, and many other animals.

South Dakota is home to the mule deer, which likes to live in areas rich in shrubs and thickets.

Although buffalo were hunted to near extinction in the nineteenth century, today South Dakota has more than eight thousand of the shaggy beasts, more than any other state. They all live on reserves, Indian reservations, or private ranches.

For Lewis and Clark, travel up the Missouri River was slow and difficult. The muddy river's many sandbars and strong currents slowed their trip. The river that divides South Dakota today bears little resemblance to the river they saw. Four dams built during the 1950s and 1960s backed up the Missouri's water, flooding vast areas of land and creating the Lewis and Clark, Oahe, Francis Case, and Sharpe lakes. These are now the state's four largest lakes and are known as the Great Lakes of South Dakota.

A bison grazes in Wind Cave National Park. More than three hundred bison live there.

ON THE TRAIL WITH LEWIS AND CLARK

Lewis and Clark were awestruck by the magnificent wildlife on the Great Plains. They were particularly impressed by the pronghorns (above), which they called antelope. Pronghorns are the fastest animals in North America, capable of reaching speeds of sixty miles per hour. The following, written by Meriwether Lewis, is from his journal entry of September 17, 1804:

This scenery already rich, pleasing and beautiful was still farther heightened by immense herds of buffalo, deer elk and antelopes which we saw in every direction feeding on the hills and plains. I do not think I exaggerate when I estimate the number of buffalo which could be comprehended at one view to amount to 3,000. . . . The antelopes which had disappeared in a steep ravine now appeared at the distance of about three miles on the side of a ridge which passed obliquely across me and extended about four miles. So soon had these antelopes gained the distance at which they had again appeared to my view I doubted at first that they were the same that I had just surprised, but my doubts soon vanished when I beheld the rapidity of their flight along the ridge before me. It appeared rather the rapid flight of birds than the motion of quadrupeds.

SUNSHINE AND BLIZZARDS

South Dakota has some of the most extreme weather found in the United States. It has been called both the Sunshine State and the Blizzard State, and both names make sense. Temperatures in the state have reached as low as 58 degrees Fahrenheit below zero and as high as 120°F above. Sometimes it seems as if a pleasant day of 70°F happens only in one's dreams. Yet South Dakotans take pride in their harsh weather. "Say what you like about our climate," South Dakota author Kathleen Norris has written. "We say it keeps the riffraff out."

Summer days are hot, often reaching 100°F. The humidity is usually low, though, so it is not sticky and uncomfortable. Still, with the flatness and the lack of trees, there is sometimes no escaping the bright sunshine.

Winter can be even worse. Even without snow, the frigid temperatures can be dangerous, making even breathing painful. But it is the blizzards that are really treacherous. The blinding snow and the driving wind make it impossible to do anything but sit inside and listen to the raging storms outside.

South Dakotans know how to get by. One Mobridge resident explained, "You dig yourself out, and then people usually get around all right, because everybody has four-wheel drives. Even if you're out on the road when a blizzard hits, you can still drive. Just open the door a crack and keep your eye on the center line." But sometimes it is impossible to drive at all. Knowing that they might get stuck at some point, many South Dakotans keep a sleeping bag in their car all through the winter. They also have a shovel and a container of sand to dump on the ground for traction if they can't get moving. Some even carry a tin can and a candle, because a candle burning in a can will warm the inside of the car.

South Dakota's winters are harsh, averaging twenty-four to thirty inches of snowfall across the state.

Even the dirt in South Dakota is difficult. The West River plains have a soil called gumbo, which is a kind of clay that gets very sticky when wet. Walk on wet ground and you will soon find two inches of mud caked on the bottom of your shoes. It just keeps building up. And it doesn't come off when you kick your shoe against the curb. No, it stays there until it dries or until there is so much of it that it falls off from its own weight. Gumbo is particularly hazardous to people driving on dirt roads. Driving may be just fine on a gorgeous July day—until a sudden rainstorm turns the road to gumbo and traps the car.

WIND AND DUST

What really distinguishes South Dakota is the wind. No place in the Lower 48 is windier than the western Dakotas. With no trees or hills in the way, the air currents pick up speed as they move across the prairie. All around South Dakota, you see abandoned houses tilting precariously, a reminder of the ever-present wind.

It seems the wind never stops. It blows dust in the eyes and weathers the skin and turns walking into real exercise. And it makes the empty land noisy. Marjorie Clark, an early settler near Lemmon, wrote of the wind, "Really it is something awful and it hardly ever goes down. It actually blows the feathers off the chickens' backs. . . . I can't put up many pictures and things for every time the door opens they all blow off the wall. . . . It's so funny—we noticed how terrible loud everyone talks out here and now we find ourselves just shouting away at the top of our voices. We discovered it must be the wind and unless you yell you can't be heard at all."

Sometimes warm winds called chinooks blow through the Black Hills. Howling through the mountains, these winds cause sudden, extreme changes in temperature. The largest change in temperature ever recorded in

South Dakota's fierce winds are sometimes strong enough to tip over a semitruck!

the United States came during a chinook in January 1943 in the town of Spearfish. In less than two minutes, the temperature rose forty-nine degrees, from 4°F below zero to 45°F above zero.

PARCHED LAND

The average yearly rainfall throughout South Dakota is only eighteen inches, though West River often gets only twelve inches. In bad years as little as seven inches may fall, the same amount as in some desert areas.

In the early 2000s, South Dakota suffered year after year of drought. Crops were failing, and some ranchers had to sell their livestock. By 2004 the effects of the extended drought had become so dire that the U.S. government declared thirty South Dakota counties a disaster area. This allowed farmers and ranchers to get low-interest loans that would help them survive the extended dry spell.

The constant wind makes South Dakota's periodic droughts even worse. Without moisture or plant roots to hold it in place, the dirt just blows away. On November 12, 1933, a huge wind storm moved across South Dakota, picking up dirt and tumbleweeds and gravel as it went. By the time the storm hit Sioux Falls, it was a hundred miles wide and moved at sixty miles per hour. At eleven that morning, the city became as dark as midnight. The wind smashed windows, felled telephone poles, and ripped bricks from chimneys.

WATCHING OUT FOR WILDLIFE

Dry conditions can also harm wildlife. Most of North America's ducks are born in the prairie pothole region of the Dakotas and Montana. The ducks rely on the small lakes and ponds to build their nests and find food. These potholes fill up in the spring with water from melting snow. But in years with less snowfall, there are fewer ponds. And in some dry years, even if there is heavy snow, the parched ground absorbs all the water, so the ponds don't fill up. In 2004, when South Dakota was suffering from a drought, the number of breeding ducks dropped by as much as 26 percent from the previous year.

Despite the drought, in the long term ducks in South Dakota are in good shape. The state is home to millions of them. But other animals are not so fortunate. South Dakota is home to twelve species that are listed by the U.S. government as threatened or endangered. These include the whooping crane, the tallest bird in North America and one of the rarest. About two hundred whooping cranes remain in the wild today. Their numbers had dropped as their habitat disappeared and they were hunted. Today the number of whooping cranes in the world is increasing, but slowly.

Black-footed ferrets are among the most endangered animals in North America. These long skinny creatures grow up to two feet in length.

They hunt at night, sneaking down into prairie-dog holes to drag out sleeping prairie dogs, which are the mainstay of their diet. By the late 1970s black-footed ferrets were thought to be extinct. But in 1981 a small number of them were found in Wyoming. Scientists began a breeding program for the ferrets. Today about a thousand black-footed ferrets are in this breeding program, but only about eighty live in the wild. Black-footed ferrets have now been released into the wild in South Dakota. Whether they can survive will depend in large part on whether they have a good supply of prairie dogs to eat. The prairie-dog population has declined by more than 90 percent since the 1800s due to poisonings, shootings, plague, and habitat loss. Many ranchers consider prairie dogs pests. Only time will tell whether prairie dogs—and the ferrets that eat them—will survive.

Black-footed ferrets have been in North America for 100,000 years. The Sioux named them "black-faced prairie dog" and the Pawnee "ground dog."

Chapter Two

Sodbusters and Indians

South Dakota's history is as colorful as its landscape is barren. Although the state was one of the last to be settled by whites, it has provided some of America's most memorable characters—outlaws and cowboys, great warriors and hardy pioneers.

THE FIRST INHABITANTS

The first people to live in South Dakota were the Paleo-Indians. They were the descendents of people who had walked on a land bridge across the Bering Strait between what are now Russia and Alaska. The oldest evidence that Paleo-Indians lived in South Dakota are campsites from about ten thousand years ago. These people were primarily hunters, living off giant bison, mammoths, sloths, and other mammals. As the climate grew drier, these large animals died off, and the Paleo-Indians turned to hunting smaller animals, fishing, and gathering roots and berries.

The Paleo-Indians were eventually replaced by the Plains Villagers, who hunted and gardened. They planted corn and hunted bison and other creatures. The Plains Villagers lived in earth lodges constructed of wooden

Native Americans are depicted crossing the Badlands in Edward Curtis's In the Bad Lands.

29

frameworks with mud for walls. They often lived in large towns, probably for protection. One such site, just outside present-day Mitchell, is about a thousand years old, and experts believe that as many as one thousand people lived there.

Another group, the Mound Builders, arose in about AD 500. They lived in what is now northeastern South Dakota along Big Sioux River. The Mound Builders are named for the large earthen mounds in which they buried their dead.

THE RISE OF THE SIOUX

The tribal groups that are known today eventually emerged from the Plains Villagers. These include the Arikara, Cheyenne, Crow, and Pawnee. Then, in the early 1700s, the Sioux began moving onto the plains. They were pushed out of the Minnesota forests by the Chippewa, who had obtained guns from French traders. Without guns, the Sioux could not compete, so they moved west.

As the Sioux spread out across the plains, they split into subgroups: the Dakota, the Nakota, and the Lakota. Those who stayed in southwestern Minnesota referred to themselves as the Dakota. Those who settled in eastern South Dakota became the Nakota. And those who moved west of the Missouri River called themselves the Lakota.

Sioux women ruled the family and life in the tepee. Above, Sioux Village, *by George Catlin.*

When the Sioux moved from forest to plains, their way of life changed dramatically. They acquired horses and went from eating berries and small animals to surviving almost exclusively off the buffalo hunt. Buffalo provided them with everything they needed. They ate the meat, made soup from the blood, and used the hides for clothing and tepees. Sinew became thread, bones made excellent tools and utensils, the tails could even be used as fly swatters. In a few short decades, the Sioux became known as the greatest warriors, hunters, and horsemen on the plains. They were brave, fearless, generous, and honorable, and they dominated the vast grasslands.

Horses brought to North America by the Spanish in the early 1500s became an important resource for the Sioux, as can be seen in The Buffalo Hunter *by Seth Eastman.*

WHITE BUFFALO CALF WOMAN

Here is a story about how the Lakota came to rely on the buffalo.

One summer long ago, the Lakota people were starving because the hunters could not find any game. But then one day, far off in the distance they saw a figure approaching. It was a beautiful young woman with dark, sparkling eyes, eyes that left no doubt about the power behind them. The woman wore a glimmering white buckskin outfit embroidered with exquisite quill work.

The woman told the Lakota that she brought something holy: the sacred pipe. She unwrapped the pipe and showed it to the people. She showed them how to smoke the pipe, what songs to sing when they filled it, and how to lift it to the sky and then in each of the four directions.

She explained that by holding the pipe toward the sky, you become a bridge between the sacred ground and the sacred heavens. This symbolizes how everything—the earth, the sky, plants, animals, and humans—are related, are one.

When she had taught the Lakota all they needed to know, the woman walked off in the same direction from which she came. As she walked she rolled over four times. The first time, she turned into a black buffalo. The second time, a brown buffalo. The third time, a red buffalo. And the fourth time, she turned into a young white female buffalo.

The moment the little white buffalo disappeared over the horizon, great herds of buffalo appeared in her place. These buffalo allowed themselves to be killed so that the Lakota would survive. And from then on, the buffalo supplied the people with everything they needed: meat for food, skins for clothing and tepees, and bones for tools. A white buffalo was the most sacred thing you could ever see.

WHITE MEN ARRIVE

Just as the Sioux were coming to power, the first European explorers entered the Dakotas. In 1743 two French brothers, François and Louis-Joseph de La Vérendrye, made their way to the upper Missouri River. When they returned east, they left behind a lead plate claiming the area for France, but this certainly didn't affect the area's native inhabitants.

When Lewis and Clark passed through the area in 1804, most of their encounters with the Indians were friendly. But as the nineteenth century progressed, trappers, traders, and settlers moved into the territory, and skirmishes between Indians and whites became more common. The Indians required huge tracts of land for their buffalo hunts. To the whites, the Indians were in the way.

The newcomers knew that to get rid of the natives they had only to get rid of the buffalo. Without buffalo, the Indians would starve, and they would have no choice but to move to the reservations as the whites wanted. General Philip Sheridan prodded hunters to slaughter "until the buffalo are exterminated" because "then your prairies can be covered with speckled cattle and the festive cowboy."

Slaughter they did. In the 1860s and 1870s, the railroads ran special trains for buffalo-hunting trips. The record for a single hunter was 120 buffalo killed in just 40 minutes. Before 1800 there were an estimated 60 million buffalo on

This 1870 woodcut shows how buffalo were slaughtered by hunters on trains.

the Great Plains. By 1889 there were just 541 of these shaggy animals left in the entire United States.

In 1868, when Red Cloud's War, a conflict between the United States and the Sioux over control of native hunting grounds, ended, the United States and the Sioux agreed to the Fort Laramie Treaty. This treaty established the Great Sioux Reservation, which included the Black Hills and all territory west from the Missouri River in the Dakotas to the Bighorn Mountains in western Wyoming. The treaty stated that the U.S. Army would protect the Great Sioux Reservation from white settlement. But this was not to be.

Fort Laramie was a major trading post and military outpost. Many of the campaigns in the Indian Wars were planned here. The Fort Laramie Treaty was named for this fort.

THE LEGEND OF HUGH GLASS

Nearly everyone has heard of such fabled characters as Wild Bill Hickok and Calamity Jane. But another legendary character, Hugh Glass, is hardly known. He embodied the fierceness and tenacity of the trappers who were the first whites in the Dakotas.

Hugh Glass was scouting one day when he came upon a grizzly. The giant bear rushed him, and soon man and bear were wrestling on the ground. Hugh's hunting party heard his screams and found him mauled and bleeding but still alive. The bear was dead. Hugh's companions didn't expect him to live long, with all his gashes, wounds, and broken bones. All they could do was dig his grave and wait for him to die.

After two days, the party moved on, except for two men who stayed behind to bury Hugh. They waited and waited, but Hugh lingered, unconscious, unable to move, unable to speak, yet still breathing. After six days, the men decided to leave: Hugh was getting no better. Undoubtedly he would die eventually, and they didn't want to die with him.

But Hugh didn't die. Eventually he woke up. Barely able to move, he looked around. He couldn't believe his companions had left him there with no food, no weapons, nothing.

Hugh vowed revenge. He would survive. He would find those men who had left him to die. He would make them look him in the eye and explain why they had left him.

So Hugh started crawling across the desolate territory. He drank water from mud puddles. He ate berries and insects and anything else he could find. It was two hundred miles to Fort Kiowa on the Missouri River, but after two months Hugh made it. Eventually he found the men who had deserted him. And he forgave them.

THE GOLD RUSH

In 1848, Father Pierre-Jean De Smet had visited the Lakota in the Black Hills. When they showed him some gold they had found, he told them, "Put it away and show it to nobody." But inevitably the secret got out. In 1874, General George Armstrong Custer led an expedition into the hills. Although he was supposed to be simply gathering information about the region, he was also looking for gold. And he found it. Almost immediately, headlines in a Chicago newspaper trumpeted that gold had been discovered in the Black Hills.

Miners poured into the hills, ignoring that it was part of the Great Sioux Reservation. The government tried to convince the Lakota to sell the hills, but the Indians refused. They believed the Black Hills were sacred; they would never give them up. So the government began a "sell or starve" policy, trying to force them into submission. Although the treaty had said the government was to supply the Indians on the reservation with food and money, Congress cut off their rations until they agreed to give up the Black Hills.

Pierre-Jean De Smet was a Jesuit missionary who befriended native tribes in the western United States. The city of De Smet was named after him.

General George Custer, best known for his involvement at the Battle of Little Bighorn, announced his discovery of gold in 1874 in the Black Hills.

Led by Sitting Bull and Crazy Horse, the Sioux fought to keep their land. They defeated Custer and his troops in the Battle of Little Bighorn in June 1876. Before the end of the year, however, the Indian resistance had been crushed, and the Sioux signed an agreement giving up the Black Hills.

The ultimate tragedy for the Sioux came on December 29, 1890. Chief Big Foot and a band of about three hundred Sioux, mostly women, children, and the elderly, were surrounded by the U.S. Cavalry near Wounded Knee Creek, on the Pine Ridge Indian Reservation. The cavalry intended to take the warriors prisoner. Because the Sioux had been traveling for weeks in the freezing winter and were cold and exhausted, they put up no struggle.

As the soldiers were disarming the Sioux, who had nothing but a few ancient rifles, a shot was fired. The cavalry then opened fire—on the warriors, on the Indians' camp, on everyone. Unarmed women and children who fled across the countryside were hunted down. When silence returned, about two hundred Sioux lay dead on the ground, turning the snow red with blood. A few days later their bodies were buried in a mass grave. Today above this grave a simple stone pillar lists the names of the Sioux who were slaughtered at Wounded Knee.

The Wounded Knee Massacre was the last major violent confrontation between the U.S. Army and the Native Americans. It buried any hope that the native people could sustain their way of life. According to historian Patrick Cudmore, the Wounded Knee Massacre "symbolizes more than just the massacre of Chief Big Foot's ragged band, more than just the ending of America's Indian Wars, and more than just the closing of America's 'last frontier.' The deeper meaning of the Wounded Knee Massacre is that it symbolized the end of almost four hundred years of unrelenting war against the indigenous people of the Americas."

A small group of Sioux who survived the Wounded Knee Massacre pose beside their tepees in 1891.

DEAD MAN'S HAND

After gold was discovered in the Black Hills, Deadwood grew from a cluster of a few shacks to a booming town of seven thousand people in just a few months. Nowhere was the Wild West wilder. The town was full of outlaws, gamblers, prospectors, and other unsavory types, and everybody was trying to make a quick buck. Into Deadwood rode and strode many of the most infamous characters of the Wild West.

Probably none were as famous as Wild Bill Hickok. Hickok had been a hunter, soldier, scout, and sheriff. But he came to Deadwood because he heard there was plenty of money to be made at the poker tables.

Some people in Deadwood were happy to see him because he had cleaned up the rough Kansas towns of Hays and Abilene. They thought maybe he could do the same thing for Deadwood. But they would be disappointed.

Not long after Hickok got to town, he made a crucial mistake. He sat in a saloon playing poker with his back to the door. A thug named Jack McCall walked in and shot him in the back of the head. Hickok fell across the table, revealing his hand, a pair of black aces and a pair of black eights, which would forever be known as the dead man's hand.

"THE DREARY BLACK HILLS"

This song is the lament of a gold miner during the gold rush. It first appeared in print around 1875, "as sung by Dick Brown." At the time there was no boundary between Wyoming and the Dakota Territory, and the Black Hills belonged to the Sioux. Dick Brown was a banjo player and singer who performed at the Melodeon, a saloon and gambling hall in Deadwood.

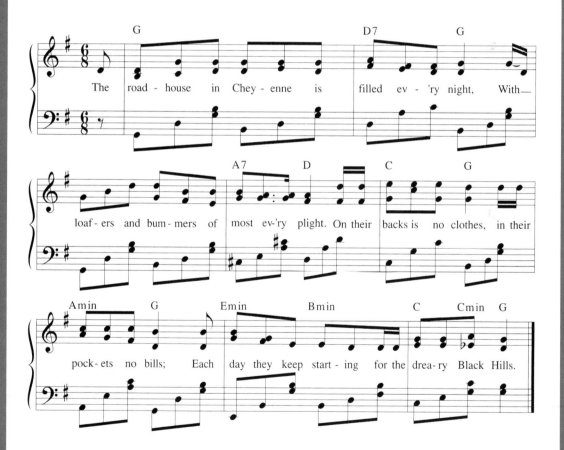

Kind friends, you must pity my horrible tale,
An object of pity, I'm looking quite stale,
I gave up my trade selling Wright's Patent Pills
To go hunting gold in the dreary Black Hills.

Chorus:
Don't go away, stay at home if you can,
Stay away from that city, they call it Cheyenne,
For a big Wallipee or Comanche Bill,
They will lift up your hair on the dreary Black Hills.

I got to Cheyenne, no gold could I find,
I thought of the lunch route I'd left far behind;
Through rain, hail, and snow, frozen plumb to the gills,
They call me the orphan of the dreary Black Hills.

Kind friend, to conclude, my advice I'll unfold,
Don't go to the Black Hills a hunter for gold;
Railroad speculators their pockets you'll fill
By taking a trip to those dreary Black Hills.

Final Chorus:
Don't go away, stay at home if you can,
Stay away from that city, they call it Cheyenne,
For old Sitting Bull or Comanche Bill
They will take off your scalp on the dreary Black Hills.

"PROVING UP"

Settlers had begun trickling into Dakota Territory after Congress passed the Homestead Act in 1862. The act gave 160 acres of land to anyone who built a shack on his claim, grew crops, and lived there for five years.

Sometimes the hardest thing about "proving up," as gaining ownership of the land was called, was building the homestead shack. In most of South Dakota, homesteaders could look in every single direction without seeing a single tree. So unless they lived next to a river, where there might be trees, log cabins were out of the question. Some people who did find wood built tar-paper-and-board shanties. But the black tar paper made the shacks unbearably hot in the summer. And because the huts were little more than cardboard, they often blew away in the persistent Dakota wind. Another option was a dugout, a shelter literally dug into the side of a hill, like a cave. Dugouts, however, sometimes collapsed.

The most popular form of homestead dwelling was the sod house, or soddy. Soddies were made by cutting large blocks of earth from the land and using them to build a house. They were sturdier than other kinds of shacks, and they were cool in the summer and warm in the winter. But they did have their problems. Sometimes the walls leaked. Other times the floors turned to mud. And then there were the unexpected dinner guests—snakes that emerged from the walls and slithered across the ceiling.

Building living quarters was only the beginning of the battle for the homesteaders. To prove up, they had to stay on it for five years. For the settlers to stay five years, their crops had to survive. But having a successful wheat or corn harvest in South Dakota is an uncertain proposition any year, and doing it five years in a row practically took a miracle. If drought didn't destroy the crops, then hail would. If the summer passed without a cloud of grasshoppers descending and chewing the crops to the ground in a day, then

Since stone and wood were hard to find, early pioneers constructed homes using sod. Those who could find wood built tar-paper-and-board shanties.

a tornado might touch down and do the job in a few seconds. Given all this, it's not surprising that only about 40 percent of homesteaders proved up.

Still, people tried. Newspapers, railroads, and land agents lured settlers to the territory. As the railroad companies built their lines west, they established towns every few miles along the routes. Where once there had been nothing but grass, towns sprang up overnight. But they left a lot to be desired. Laura Ingalls Wilder wrote of De Smet, "The town was like a sore on the beautiful, wild prairie. Old haystacks and manure piles were rotting around the stables, the backs of the stores' false fronts were rough and ugly. . . . The town smelled of staleness and dust and smoke and a fatty odor of cooking."

Even so, people came in droves to what newspapers told them was the "sole remaining quarter-section of paradise in the western world." Between 1870 and 1890, the population of South Dakota increased 3,000 percent, from 11,800 to 348,600. But many settlers faced bitter disappointment.

Another difficult aspect of homesteading was the absolute isolation of life on the prairie, where the nearest neighbor might be miles away. Eliza Jane Wilder, a pioneer in eastern South Dakota and the sister-in-law of Laura Ingalls Wilder, wrote in 1880, "The utter silence and loneliness grew so terrible as to be almost unendurable. I think I fathomed the depth of the word Alone." One sodbuster (farmer) in ten was a woman. Sometimes, to ward off the devastating loneliness, sisters staked neighboring claims and worked their fields together. Occasionally they even built their homestead shacks right next to each other, one on either side of the property line.

Whether the settlers were related or not, they relied on their neighbors, both to keep from going crazy and to help them in times of need. Home-steader Edward Boyden wrote, "There are hardships to struggle with that would make strong men weak and weak men stagger. At times you got so tired you could trip sitting down. . . . It would be so much harder if it weren't for your good neighbors. . . . The only time one would spit in a neighbor's face was if his mustache was on fire."

Eventually the government realized that 160 acres was simply not enough land for survival in dry climates. So in 1909 Congress passed the Enlarged Homestead Act, which made homesteads 320 acres in states with less than fifteen inches of rain per year. But the people in charge in South Dakota didn't want potential settlers to know how dry it actually was in "the sole remaining paradise," so the state did not comply with this act until 1915.

POPULATION GROWTH: 1870–2000

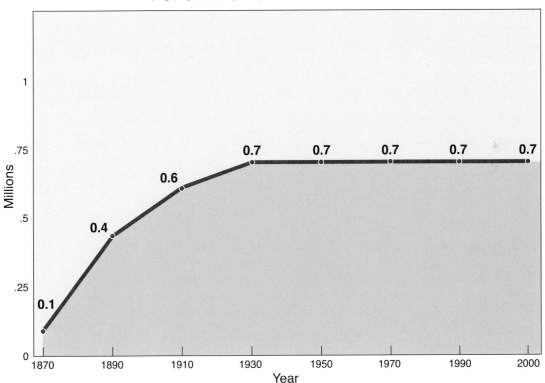

STATEHOOD

As Dakota Territory's population increased in the 1870s and 1880s, people began clamoring for statehood. In 1889 their cries were heard, and North and South Dakota were created. President Benjamin Harrison shuffled the documents admitting the two states before he signed them on November 2, 1889, so no one will ever know for sure whether South Dakota is the thirty-ninth state or the fortieth. Because North Dakota comes first alphabetically, South Dakota is called the fortieth state. Although Pierre was small and out of the way, it was declared the capital because it was the town closest to the center of the state.

HARD TIMES

Life never became easy for the farmers and ranchers of South Dakota. Blizzards, grasshoppers, and drought continued to plague them. The drought of 1910–1911 was particularly bad, forcing many people off the land. While going to visit a friend seventeen miles from his home, one farmer, Oscar Micheaux, passed forty-seven houses. "Only one had an occupant," he reported.

Drought was even worse in the 1930s, when dust storms blew away much of the land. During this time, when much of the Midwest became known as the dust bowl, several billion tons of topsoil blew off the Great Plains. The price of wheat had gone up dramatically during the 1910s, so farmers had plowed under more and more of the prairie grasses. When severe drought hit in 1932, the soil blew away because there were no grass and roots to hold the dirt in place. Some of the dust storms dropped dirt as far away as the Atlantic Ocean. The drought continued throughout the decade, and many farmers watched their land turn into desert.

Sand drifts up to six feet deep sometimes formed along farmhouses during the dust bowl.

Life for South Dakota's Native Americans was harder still. For many it was a downward spiral of poverty, alcoholism, neglect, and abuse. In the 1970s some Sioux tried to change things. Members of a civil rights organization called the American Indian Movement (AIM) went to Pine Ridge Indian Reservation in 1973. The reservation by this time was a miserable place. Not only were the living conditions appalling, but the tribal government was corrupt. The tribal president, Richard "Dickie" Wilson, controlled a group of thugs who terrorized the residents.

In February about three hundred AIM members, Lakotas, and supporters from other tribes took over the town of Wounded Knee.

A member of the American Indian Movement protests at Wounded Knee for better living conditions and a fair tribal government.

They were protesting the conditions on the reservation, the breaking of the 1868 Fort Laramie Treaty, corruption in the Bureau of Indian Affairs, and the routine violence and discrimination suffered by Native Americans in the area. The Federal Bureau of Investigation, federal marshals, and Wilson's thugs surrounded the town. The standoff lasted seventy-one days, until the government agreed to discuss the Fort Laramie Treaty with the Sioux.

In 1980 the U.S. Supreme Court ruled that the federal government had illegally taken the Black Hills from the Sioux. The Fort Laramie Treaty stated that no changes could be made in the treaty without the written approval of 75 percent of the adult Sioux males. But the 1876 agreement in which the Sioux gave up the Black Hills had been signed by only 10 percent. The Supreme Court concluded that because the government had wanted the Black Hills gold to be mined, it had tried to starve the Sioux and then forced a small group of them to sign the agreement. "A more ripe and rank case of dishonorable dealings will never, in all probability, be found in our history," the Court said in its ruling.

The Court awarded the Sioux more than $100 million in damages. But like their ancestors a century before, they refused the money. What they want is the land.

TO THE FUTURE

The 1980s were rough times for South Dakota. Low farm prices and high interest rates forced many farmers off their land. Though it was difficult, South Dakotans began focusing on diversifying the state's economy. In 1981 Citibank moved its credit-card operation to Sioux Falls, and South Dakota was on its way to becoming a leader in the service economy. In 1989 the state legalized casino gambling in Deadwood, the legendary Wild West town in the Black Hills. Tourists poured in to enjoy the slot machines and blackjack tables, and taxes on gambling became an important source of revenue for the state.

Though tourists spend much of their time looking back at South Dakota's lively history, South Dakotans themselves are looking forward. The state is looking at giving the former Homestake gold mine—the deepest mine in the United States—to the National Science Foundation, which would use it to build a unique underground science laboratory. South Dakotans will continue to look at ways to broaden their economy, and build a better future for themselves and their children.

Chapter Three
A Small-Town World

In South Dakota, East River and West River are more than just geographic areas. They also define people. East River is thought to be home to urban and conventional people, whereas West River has a lot of rough, independent-minded folk. But many South Dakotans scoff at this alleged divide. "Nah, there's not much difference," said a woman who had moved from Sioux Falls, the heart of East River, to distant Spearfish, in West River. "People here have been real nice to us."

TOWNS AND NEIGHBORS

On both sides of the Missouri, South Dakota is defined by its small towns. The state's largest city, Sioux Falls, has only 136,695 residents, and the second largest, Rapid City, has about 61,000. After that, the size of towns quickly dwindles.

Most people who live in South Dakota's small towns are happy to be there. They like the quality of life, the neighborliness. "I hope we can preserve some of this," said Dennis Menke, owner of a store in Yankton. "That's the thing about America, we're so set on always *changing* things.

No matter their background, most South Dakotans take pride in their heritage and state.

Well, I'm not." Menke believes that small-town life forces people to treat each other decently. "We try to think long term with people, give them a little extra care," he said. "You can't just scoot people in and out the door and take advantage of 'em. In a small town like this, you'd be through in a year."

The neighborly hospitality that pioneers needed to survive has continued to this day. In South Dakota, people are expected to be friendly and helpful. After bicycling through the state, Bruce Weber was pleased to report, "Drivers going the other way wave from behind the wheel . . . and residents . . . seem to be of a particularly gregarious American stripe."

But small towns have their disadvantages, too. Often they can't provide everything their residents need. Mobridge, for instance, which has about four thousand people, has only one women's dress shop. But the clothes are too expensive for some people, so they have to drive two hours to Aberdeen or Pierre to find more options.

Small-town life can be particularly hard on the poor because they are isolated from the services that can help them. In western South Dakota, people may have to travel a hundred miles or more to register for unemployment benefits. If they have no car, they're out of luck: there are no buses or trains to take them.

MOVING AWAY

Though South Dakota is still a small-town world, this is slowly changing. Every ten years, the United States conducts a census, counting all the people in the country. The 2000 census was the first one in which more people in South Dakota lived in urban areas than in rural areas. Part of this is the result of the changing economy. Farming is no longer the dominant business in the state. Fewer families now live on farms, so the businesses in the small towns that once served those farms have fewer customers.

Small-town charm is well preserved throughout South Dakota.

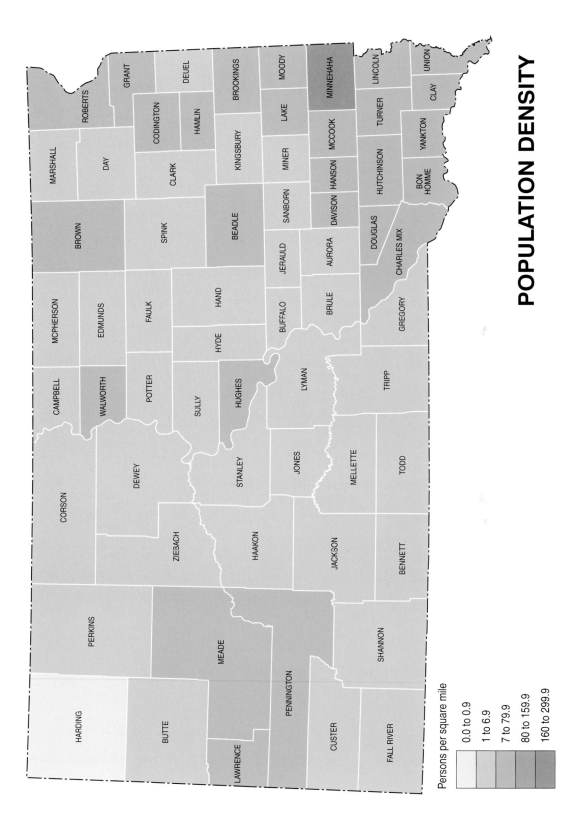

POPULATION DENSITY

Persons per square mile

- 0.0 to 0.9
- 1 to 6.9
- 7 to 79.9
- 80 to 159.9
- 160 to 299.9

Some of these businesses can't keep afloat, so people are forced to move to larger cities such as Sioux Falls to find work. Many young people leave the state entirely. Some go to places such as Minneapolis, Minnesota, in search of the job opportunities and culture that only big cities can provide.

Evidence of these changes is everywhere. About two-thirds of the schools in South Dakota have a shrinking number of students. In rural areas, there are more deaths each year than births. And every year, more native-born Americans leave South Dakota than move there.

But many residents of small South Dakota towns wouldn't consider living anywhere else. "There's less congestion, less crime, less pollution," said one man. For many people, the small-town lifestyle is reason enough to stay. "It's peaceful here, and my property taxes are under a hundred dollars a year," said postmaster Ellen Speck of Gann Valley. "And I can see the stars at night and see the sun go up and down."

HITTING THE ROAD

South Dakotans love to drive. A motorcyclist races down the twisted roads through the Black Hills. A lone pickup cruises the rolling plains of the northwest. A businessman is so used to the empty stretches of a straight-as-an-arrow highway that he reads a newspaper while he's driving! For all three, South Dakota's deserted roads offer pleasant relaxation. "Among the simple pleasures of Dakota is driving where there's no traffic," wrote Kathleen Norris, recalling the evening she drove two hundred miles from Rapid City to Lemmon and saw fewer than fifteen cars but more than one hundred antelope.

But driving in South Dakota has its problems: you are in the world of small towns, a world where businesses close in the evening and people go home to their families. Late-night gas stations are few and far

South Dakota's scenic byways attract thousands of motorcyclists each year.

between, sometimes as much as two hundred miles apart. The first piece of advice given to any traveler to South Dakota is to fill up your tank whenever you can.

One thing all South Dakotans seem to love is sports. "That's pretty much all anyone around here does," said one Aberdeen woman. They play basketball, baseball, and football with a passion. Hunting and fishing are ways of life. At various times of the year, hunters stalk pheasants, grouse, geese, ducks, deer, and antelope. From huge Lake Oahe to a tiny stream in the Black Hills, fishermen wait for a bite from walleyes, catfish, trout, or sturgeon.

HARLEYS IN THE HILLS

West River people love motorcycles. It is not uncommon to see nice-looking middle-aged couples on motorcycles, complete with headsets so that they can talk to each other. There's something about the landscape that makes people want to get on their bikes and roar off into the sunset.

That roar is loudest in the small town of Sturgis, just on the edge of the Black Hills. Every August more than 500,000 people on Harley-Davidsons converge on Sturgis for the world's largest motorcycle rally. During that week they hold drag races, hill climbs, road tours, and motorcycle rodeos. They also enjoy rock concerts and admire each other's bikes. Basically it's a weeklong party. If you want a motel room or don't like noise, stay far away. If you ever fall in love with motorcycles, though, you might find yourself in Sturgis.

ETHNIC SOUTH DAKOTA

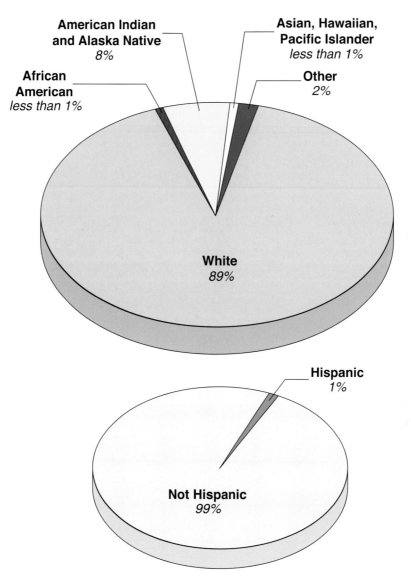

American Indian
and Alaska Native
8%

Asian, Hawaiian,
Pacific Islander
less than 1%

African
American
less than 1%

Other
2%

White
89%

Hispanic
1%

Not Hispanic
99%

Note: A person of Cuban, Mexican, Puerto Rican, South or Central American, or other Spanish culture or origin, regardless of race, is defined as Hispanic.

CELEBRATING THE PAST

South Dakota's population is predominately white. About 88.7 percent of the population can trace their origins to Europe. Native Americans are the next largest group, making up about 8.3 percent of the population.

Many of the state's early pioneers were foreigners. In 1920, 28 percent of South Dakota's population had been born abroad. Back in the early days of the state, Germans, Swedes, Norwegians, and many others came in droves. Some ended up in small towns dominated by their own ethnic group. Today these places celebrate their heritage with summer festivals. For instance, each June thousands of people pour into Tabor, a tiny town of four hundred, to enjoy Czech Days. During the two-day celebration, they dance the polka, eat tarts called *kolaces*, and recall what they can of the language spoken by their immigrant parents and grandparents.

Czechs celebrate their heritage. Some by preparing kolaces, *sweet pastries stuffed with various fillings.*

Many other towns have festivals and rodeos celebrating their pioneer or Wild West heritage. Every summer De Smet holds the Laura Ingalls Wilder Pageant, which features demonstrations of pioneer skills such as quilting and butter churning, as well as a performance that re-creates events from her books. "We feel we're trying to preserve the history and authenticity of Laura Ingalls Wilder," said Donna Bierschbach, who is in charge of publicity for the pageant.

PROUD TRADITIONS

The various Indian reservations throughout the state host annual powwows featuring traditional dancing, crafts, and food. These events preserve and celebrate Native American culture and are enjoyed by all.

After suffering so many years of attack, the Lakotas are now doing everything they can to preserve their culture—to maintain the old ways and to remember who they are. Some of this knowledge is passed on at the many tribal colleges that have recently sprung up on reservations. "This is one of the most wonderful revolutions in Indian Country, the right to educate on our own terms," explained Dr. David Gipp of the American Indian Higher Education Consortium. At Sinte Gleska University on the Rosebud Reservation, in the southern part of the state, all students are required to study the Lakota language. This is as different as can be from the old government boarding schools, where children were forbidden to speak their native languages and were taught that their culture was inferior.

Guy Dull Knife Jr., who grew up on the Pine Ridge Indian Reservation, believes that it is necessary for the Lakota to function in the white world *and* to maintain their own traditions. He said, "If we are to make it as a people, our children must know about computers and the Eagle Dance. They must know the value of earning a living and about our traditional relationship with the earth. They need to know how to read and write and balance a checkbook, but they must also know who they are and where they came from. It is our job to teach them these things, just like our fathers before us. Then it will be up to them to help their children learn the ways of both the white world and the Indian world."

Sioux dancers retain their traditions and heritage on the Pine Ridge Reservation.

INDIAN TACOS

South Dakotans love simple, all-American food: hamburgers, steak, eggs. But one interesting variation that has grown popular in recent years is the Indian taco. It combines a traditional Indian dish called fry bread with the regular ingredients of a taco to create a quick, filling, and delicious meal. Have an adult help you with this recipe.

1 1/2 pounds hamburger
salt
pepper
1/2 pound cheddar cheese
3 medium tomatoes
1 small head of lettuce
2 1/2 cups flour
1 teaspoon salt
3 teaspoons baking powder
1/2 teaspoon sugar
1 cup warm milk
1/4 cup vegetable oil
1 pint sour cream

In a large frying pan, brown hamburger until thoroughly cooked. Add a dash of salt and pepper. Grate the cheese, and chop the tomatoes and lettuce.

To make fry bread, combine the remaining dry ingredients. Add warm milk and 1 teaspoon oil, and mix into dough. Divide and shape dough into eight flat pancakes. Heat remaining oil over medium heat. Fry dough in oil until brown and crispy.

On each hot fry bread put some hamburger, cheese, tomato, lettuce, and a dollop of sour cream. Eat with a fork. Enjoy!

THE CHANGING FACE OF SOUTH DAKOTA

Although South Dakota is still mostly white and Native American, the number of people from other ethnic groups is growing. Today immigrants to the state are more likely to be from Latin America, Africa, or Asia than from Europe. Many immigrants have settled in Sioux Falls, the state's largest city. They have come from the Philippines, Vietnam, Lebanon, Ethiopia, and many other places. Many come to make a better life for themselves. Others are escaping the horrors back home. About two thousand Sudanese refugees live in the Sioux Falls area. Many were small children when war erupted in the Sudan in the 1980s. Today they are trying to find their way in a strange world thousands of miles from where they grew up.

Huron, a town of about 12,000 people in the eastern part of the state, is seeing a large influx of people from Mexico, Guatemala, and other Spanish-speaking countries. Many of the newcomers to Huron work in the city's turkey and beef plants. Mexican grocery stores and other businesses that cater to the new immigrants have sprung up in Huron. School enrollment is also rising. It's expected that the percentage of minority kids in the schools will shoot up from 2 percent to 10 percent in just a few years. Many old-time residents of Huron are happy to meet the newcomers from far-flung places. "It helps us open our eyes a little bit to the rest of the world," said one local nurse. A number of Huron residents are taking Spanish-language classes. Most will never learn to speak the language well, but at least they'll be able to say hello to their new neighbors.

Chapter Four

Public Life

Running a society requires organization. There have to be laws that people agree upon, methods of collecting money to build roads and schools, courts to interpret how the laws should be applied, and ways for citizens to influence their world.

INSIDE GOVERNMENT

The government of South Dakota is based on its state constitution, which was adopted in 1889. South Dakota's constitution has been changed, or amended, more than eighty times. The South Dakota constitution divides the government into three branches: executive, legislative, and judicial.

Executive

The executive branch is headed by the governor, who has many duties. Most important, the governor must sign any bill passed by the legislature for it to become law. Governors also focus attention on issues they think are important, call special sessions of the legislature, and appoint high-ranking officials. The governor is elected to a four-year term but cannot serve more than two terms in a row.

Completed in 1910, South Dakota's capitol building in Pierre features Capitol Lake, a favorite resting place for the area's waterfowl.

South Dakota's governor, Mike Rounds, took office in 2003.

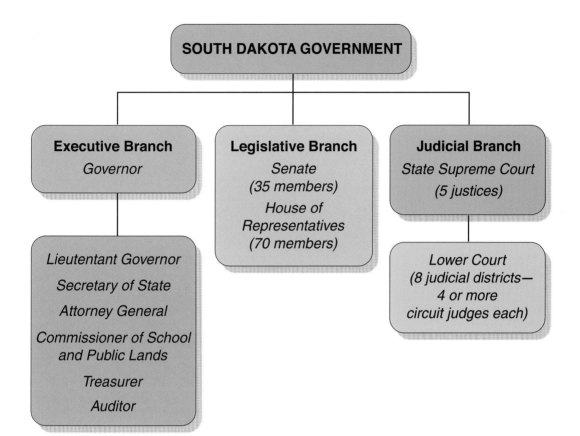

SOUTH DAKOTA GOVERNMENT

Executive Branch
Governor

Lieutentant Governor

Secretary of State

Attorney General

Commissioner of School and Public Lands

Treasurer

Auditor

Legislative Branch
Senate (35 members)

House of Representatives (70 members)

Judicial Branch
State Supreme Court (5 justices)

Lower Court (8 judicial districts— 4 or more circuit judges each)

Legislative

The legislative branch of government makes laws and passes budgets. The South Dakota legislature is made up of a thirty-five-member senate and a seventy-member house. Legislators' terms are two years, and they may serve no more than four terms in a row. South Dakota's legislators are not professional politicians. In fact, the legislature meets for only three months annually, making the capital of Pierre a lonely place for much of the year. The rest of the time, senators and representatives are farmers and businesspeople, lawyers and housewives.

South Dakota's legislators make and pass laws in the capitol building.

Judicial

South Dakota's judicial system is headed by the state supreme court. The court rules on whether laws have been applied correctly and whether new laws passed by the legislature violate the state constitution. The court consists of five justices, each appointed by the governor. Three years after the justices are appointed, the people of the state vote on whether to retain them. Thereafter, justices must be reapproved by a statewide vote every eight years.

An attorney presents his case to South Dakota's Supreme Court justices.

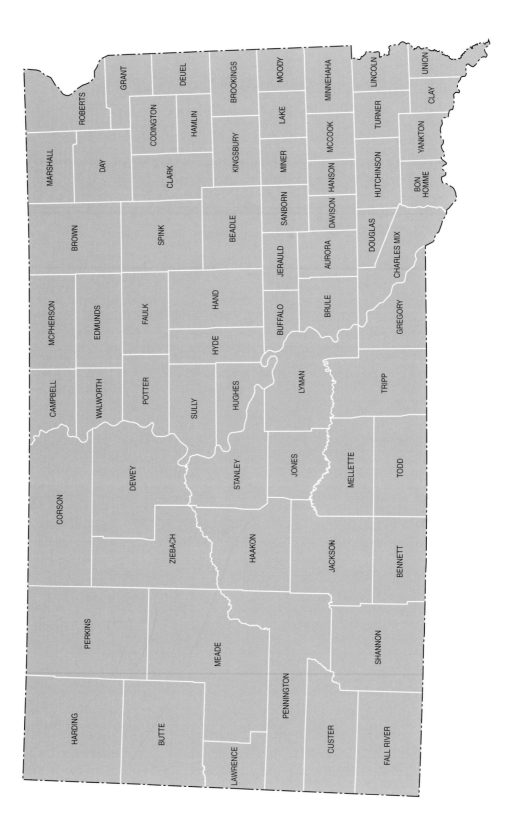

SOUTH DAKOTA BY COUNTY

MAKING LAWS

The South Dakota government deals with a huge variety of issues. When Mike Rounds was running for governor in 2002, he expressed much concern over the number of young people leaving the state. After he was elected, he proposed a bill to start the "Dakota Corps" scholarship program as a way of encouraging young people to stay. Students who agreed to stay in the state after graduation and work in certain vital jobs such as teaching and nursing would get free college tuition funded by a coalition of private and public agencies. Many state legislators liked the idea of the scholarships, but they could not agree on details of the program, so the bill did not pass. But Rounds sought out private contributions to fund the scholarships, and today the program is up and running.

Lawmakers have other issues to contend with. When ranchers complained that prairie dogs were eating all their grass, leaving little for their cows to graze on, lawmakers in Pierre decided to help them out. In 2005 they passed a law saying that prairie dogs could be treated as pests, just as mice and rats are. This made it possible for county pest-control boards to poison the prairie dogs, but this is a controversial issue between conservationists and businesses.

THE PEOPLE SPEAK

The citizens of South Dakota have always been very active in governing their state. South Dakota was the first state to adopt the initiative and the referendum, two methods for citizens to directly influence which laws are enacted. In an initiative, if enough people sign a petition requesting that a certain law be adopted, then it is put on the ballot in the next election. If a majority of the citizens vote for it, the ballot

A South Dakotan enters a polling station during the 2004 election.

measure becomes law. In a referendum, people sign petitions asking that an existing law be put on the ballot for the public's approval. If the majority vote yes at election time, the law stands; if they vote no, it is struck down.

Having initiatives and referendums on the ballot sometimes increases people's interest in the political process, making them more likely to vote. Some people believe this is one reason South Dakota has a very high voter turnout. In the 2004 elections, South Dakota had the fifth-highest turnout in the nation, with 66 percent of the voting-age population going to the polls, compared with only about 55 percent nationwide. Another reason that more South Dakotans vote may be that because the state population is so small they are likely to have met the candidates. What's more, South Dakota State University political science professor Bob Burns thinks South Dakotans vote in higher numbers because going to the polls isn't the problem it can be in some big cities. "People don't anticipate long lines to vote," he explained, "and the polls are not far away."

Chapter Five

Making a Living

South Dakota has traditionally had a boom-and-bust economy. This was because the state's economy was based on agriculture. High prices and good weather mean prosperity for farmers, but falling prices and a drought can quickly put them out of business.

FARMS AND FACTORIES

Agriculture remains an important part of South Dakota's economy. Farms and ranches stretch over nine-tenths of the state. In 2004 South Dakota was the nation's second-leading producer of sunflowers. It ranked third in production of oats and millet, fourth in rye and flaxseed, and fifth in alfalfa hay. The state is also a major supplier of corn, wheat, and cattle.

Though South Dakota is still very much a farm state, manufacturing and service industries now make up a larger part of the state's economy. Meatpacking and food processing are both important in South Dakota. The state is also a big manufacturer of computers and machinery.

In 2002 South Dakota had over 43 million acres of farmland. A leading crop is wheat, with more than 3.5 million acres planted each year.

A farmer inspects his sunflower crop. Two types of sunflowers are grown in South Dakota, oilseed (for birdseed and vegetable oil) and confectionary (for snack food).

In 1989 a free trade agreement between the United States and Canada went into effect. This agreement eliminated tariffs that had to be paid on goods traded between the two countries. In 1994 the United States also began free trade with Mexico. Since then, South Dakota's exports have been steadily rising. Canada is by far South Dakota's biggest trading partner, accounting for 43 percent of the state's exports in 2003. Mexico and Hong Kong are also major markets for South Dakota products. The state's leading exports are meat and computers.

Many South Dakotans oppose extending free-trade agreements to other countries. Goods from countries that have lower wages and other costs can be sold for less here. South Dakota's farmers and manufacturers may not be able to compete with these lower-priced goods.

2003 GROSS STATE PRODUCT: $27 Million

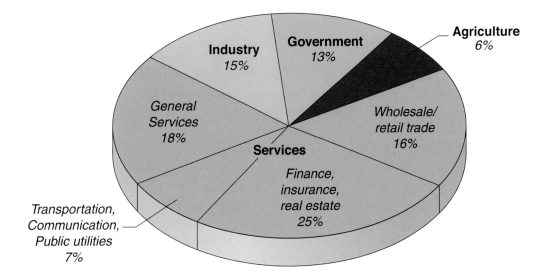

Government 13%

Agriculture 6%

Industry 15%

General Services 18%

Services

Wholesale/ retail trade 16%

Finance, insurance, real estate 25%

Transportation, Communication, Public utilities 7%

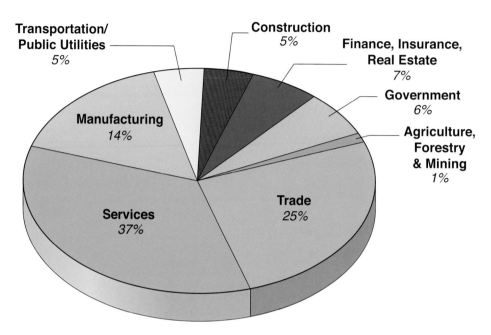

SOUTH DAKOTA WORKFORCE

Transportation/
Public Utilities
5%

Construction
5%

Finance, Insurance,
Real Estate
7%

Government
6%

Agriculture,
Forestry
& Mining
1%

Manufacturing
14%

Trade
25%

Services
37%

SERVICE INDUSTRIES

Farming began declining in South Dakota in the 1980s. Since then, more and more South Dakotans began working in service industries. Tourism has become big business in South Dakota, employing one out of every twelve workers in the state. Several million people visit South Dakota every year.

Sioux Falls is the economic center of the state. The city is also a major center for retailing, medical services, and communications. Through the 1970s, Sioux Falls was a major manufacturing center, but today one in ten employed people in Sioux Falls works at a call center. Each day these people go to work, put on a telephone headset, and answer calls from customers around the country. Citicorp, HSBC, and several other financial institutions have call centers in Sioux Falls.

Employed by the state, this park ranger inspects the condition of Mount Rushmore National Memorial.

Customer service positions, such as call center representatives in telemarketing and tele-sales, provide many jobs in South Dakota.

The rapid growth of call centers in Sioux Falls in the 1980s and 1990s helped keep people in South Dakota. "Call centers created more jobs for college graduates," said economist Ralph Brown. "More stayed here, and now there are more high-paying service jobs, and more people are staying and getting an education."

In recent years many American companies have moved their call centers to other nations, where they can pay lower wages. Today the person answering a banking question or offering computer help is often halfway around the world, in a country such as India. Many people in Sioux Falls fear that their jobs, too, will go overseas. Today Sioux Falls is trying to attract clients and jobs at call centers and other businesses that require a higher level of education. Call center jobs that require more education are less likely to go overseas.

EARNING A LIVING

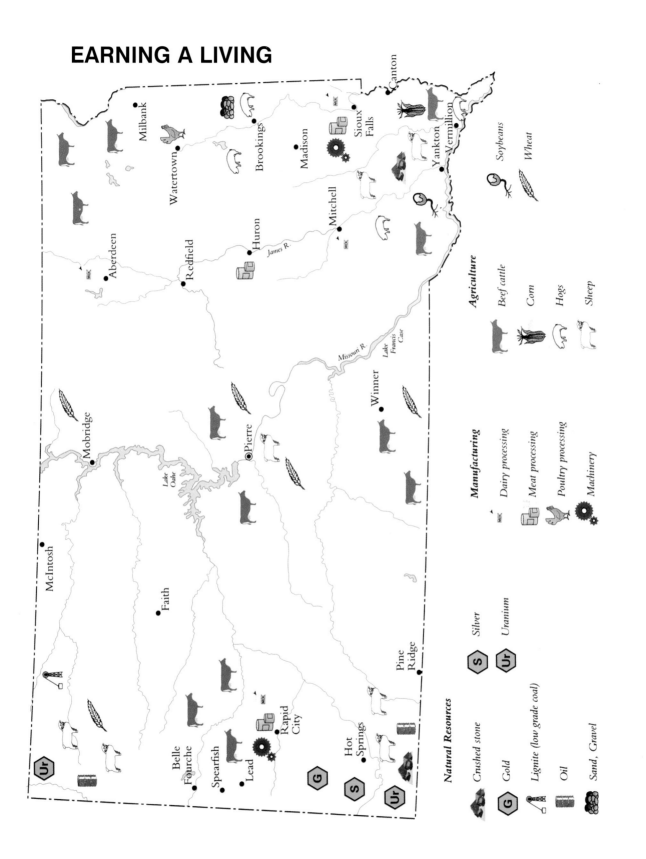

CLIMBING OUT OF POVERTY

South Dakota's economy has been healthy in the early 2000s. The state's unemployment rate is lower than the national average, and it is rated one of the best places to start a business. But some parts of the state still struggle with poverty. Shannon County, in Pine Ridge Reservation, is one of the poorest counties in the entire nation. Today, 69 percent of the people on the reservation live in poverty, compared with 12.7 percent nationwide. Despite such desperation, things are looking up. The casinos that have sprouted on so many reservations in recent years have brought in much-needed cash. Many other kinds of businesses are growing on the reservations as well, including newspapers, manufacturing, and tourism.

Though located in one of the most beautiful regions of the state, the Pine Ridge Reservation is also one of the poorest, with an average annual family income of $3,700.

In order to earn additional income, this Native American woman sells handmade jewelry and decorations.

"A lot of things have failed out here in Indian Country," said Fred Dubray, a Sioux from the Cheyenne River reservation. Until 2002 he was director of the Cheyenne River Sioux Tribe's bison program. In 2002 he became director of the Intertribal Bison Cooperative, which has a membership of more than forty tribes in several states. "So we started to think back to the days when we were self-sufficient, back to the days of the buffalo."

Dubray has built up a large herd of bison. Bison meat has become increasingly popular with American consumers because it has less fat and cholesterol than beef has. Like his ancestors, Dubray uses all parts of the buffalo. The skin becomes clothing, the bones become utensils, and the skulls are made into jewelry, which is sold in gift shops. Although Indian income has not risen much, most people believe there is more reason for hope than there has been for generations.

Chapter Six

Freeways and Byways

For many people, South Dakota is nothing but one long, straight freeway ride to the Badlands and the Black Hills. But if you take the time to get off the freeway and onto the lonely highways and byways, you will discover some fascinating places and the friendliest of people.

EASTERN SOUTH DAKOTA

In Vermillion, in the extreme southeastern corner of South Dakota, is the National Music Museum, one of the best museums of musical instruments in the world. Ask the woman at the information desk why this collection—rivaled only by those in such cultural centers as Vienna and Berlin—is here, in a place that many people would call the middle of nowhere, and she'll laugh, nod her head, and say, "That's what everybody wants to know." The museum began as the property of one very enthusiastic band teacher named Arne B. Larson, who collected more than 2,500 instruments, some of them magnificent antiques, others beat-up trash. He donated the collection to the University of South Dakota. The museum opened in 1973, and the collection has continued to grow ever since.

Needles Highway, located in Custer State Park, passes through tunnels and by rock spires. It is one of the most scenic roads in the state.

At the National Music Museum, visitors can view violin-making demonstrations.

As visitors stroll the exhibits, they often stop and marvel at an exquisite violin by Antonio Stradivari, the greatest violin maker in history. This beautiful instrument is considered by many to be the finest violin made before 1700. There is also a guitar that he made, one of the only two surviving Stradivari guitars in the world. The collection has examples of instruments from different periods, so you can see how a guitar came to look like a guitar and a saxophone like a saxophone. It also contains fascinating instruments from every corner of the globe. For instance, there is the oud, the great instrument of Arab classical music, which looks something like a mandolin with eleven strings.

For fans of Laura Ingalls Wilder's Little House books, De Smet is a must-see. It is the real "little town on the prairie," where Laura's family moved in 1879. The books *By the Shores of Silver Lake, The Long Winter, Little Town on the Prairie,* and *These Happy Golden Years* all take place in and around De Smet. Many Ingalls artifacts remain in the town. You can tour the town's oldest building, the Surveyors' House, where the family spent the winter in *By the Shores of Silver Lake.* The house that Pa built in 1887 is also open to visitors. Although Laura was already married to Almanzo Wilder by then, Ma, Pa, and Mary lived out their lives there, and the house contains items that belonged to all the Ingallses, including Laura and her only child, Rose. On the site of the Ingalls homestead, the five cottonwood trees that Pa planted in honor of his wife and four daughters still stand.

The Ingalls Homestead was chosen by Charles Ingalls for its good water and proximity to De Smet.

De Smet Cemetery contains the graves of all the Ingalls family except Laura, Almanzo, and Rose, as well as graves of other people mentioned in the books.

Mitchell is home to one of the state's oddest tourist attractions, the Corn Palace. The building gets its name from the murals that cover its exterior—murals made of corn as well as other grains and grasses. Every September the town celebrates Corn Palace Week, when the previous year's murals are removed and new ones are put up. Inside the building some of the best works are on permanent display. These were created by Sioux artist Oscar Howe, who designed the Corn Palace murals from 1948 to 1971.

The original structure was built in 1892 to help convince people that eastern South Dakota was a fertile wonderland and a great place to live. Over time, the building was expanded and embellished. It was given brightly colored towers and minarets, making it look like something out of Disneyland. At first the building was used for agricultural exhibitions. Later, big-band concerts were often held there. Today, apart from hosting tourists, it is where local basketball games are played.

Mitchell thrives on the tourists who make it their one stop off the interstate on the way to the Black Hills. The corn theme is everywhere. You know you're near the Corn Palace, and the center of town, when you see lampposts festooned with corncobs. Locals seem somewhat bemused by their town's unusual claim to fame. Ask the people who work in the palace's giant gift shop what they think of it, and more likely than not, they will roll their eyes. One young woman said, "It's no big deal. It's just corn. We see it every day. It's where we play our basketball games. Other people come and say 'Wow,' but some people think it's dumb."

Originally called "The Corn Belt Exposition," today the Corn Palace hosts shows and sporting events.

PLACES TO SEE

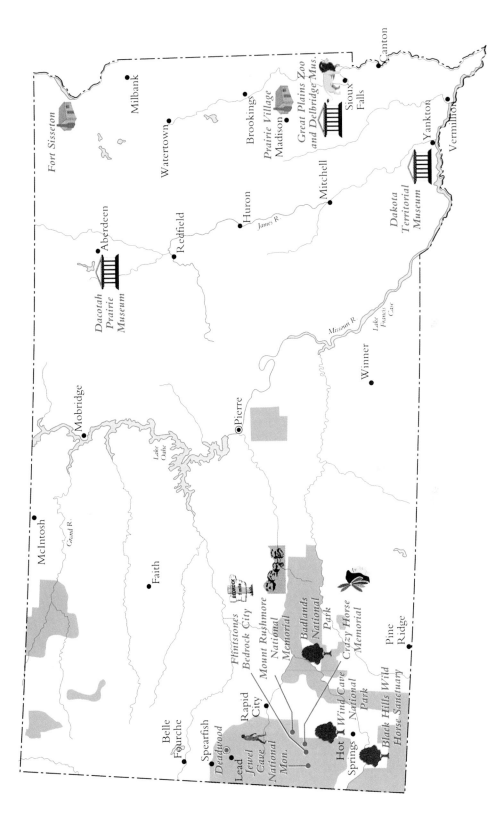

Fort Sisseton

Milbank

Watertown

Aberdeen

Dacotah
Prairie
Museum

Redfield

Huron

James R.

Brookings

Prairie Village
Madison

Great Plains Zoo and Delbridge Mus.

Sioux
Falls

Canton

Mitchell

Dakota
Territorial
Museum

Yankton

Vermillion

Missouri R.

Lake
Francis
Case

Winner

Mobridge

Pierre

Lake
Oahe

McIntosh

Grand R.

Faith

Flintstones
Bedrock City

Mount Rushmore
National
Memorial

Badlands
National
Park

Crazy Horse
Memorial

Pine
Ridge

Rapid
City

Wind Cave
National Park

Black Hills Wild
Horse Sanctuary

Belle
Fourche

Spearfish

Deadwood

Lead

Jewel
Cave
National
Mon.

Hot
Springs

Way off the interstate, not far from the North Dakota border, is Mobridge, a town that doesn't get many tourists but is well worth the visit. Just outside of town is the grave of the great Sioux leader Sitting Bull. In 1890, Sitting Bull was killed by tribal police just outside his cabin in South Dakota. His body was taken to Fort Yates in North Dakota and unceremoniously buried. In 1953 some of his descendants dug up his remains and reburied them near Mobridge, in Sitting Bull's home territory.

Today the site is marked by a large granite bust sculpted by Korczak Ziolkowski, the same artist who began work on the Crazy Horse Memorial in the Black Hills. Chances are, if you visit the grave you will be the only one there, for it is far off the beaten path. If you go in early summer, the surrounding grassland is covered with yellow flowers, and as you sit alone you can seem to hear the ancient, sorrowful voices in the steady wind.

Mobridge is also proud of its Scherr-Howe Arena. Ten murals by Oscar Howe adorn the inside. During the Great Depression in the 1930s, the federal government established the Work Projects Administration (WPA) to create jobs for people in all lines of work, including artists and writers. Howe was hired to paint the murals in the auditorium. He completed the job

The granite bust of Sitting Bull marks the grave of the leader of the Indian resistance against the U.S. Army that resulted in the Battle of the Little Bighorn.

in about six weeks for the regular WPA wage of sixty dollars per month. The murals depict the history and everyday life of the Native Americans in the area with great pride, dignity, and humanity.

About a hundred miles south of Mobridge is Pierre, the state capital. The city boasts an attractive capitol, complete with marble staircases, mosaic floors, and a shimmering dome. But Pierre's most interesting site is the Cultural Heritage Center, the state historical museum. It includes an excellent exhibit on the ways of life of the Plains Indians, including a full-size tepee, beautiful artifacts, and videos of Native Americans talking in both Lakota and English about their culture. There are also entertaining displays about the settlers who moved into South Dakota. Historical reconstructions such as a sod house make clear the hardships suffered by the pioneers.

Native culture and heritage is taught and preserved at South Dakota's Cultural Heritage Center.

THE BADLANDS

Perhaps the outstanding attraction in South Dakota is Badlands National Park. With its unearthly spires, gullies, and ridges of ever-changing hues, it is truly a national treasure. At midday, the bright sunshine washes out some of the color in the hills. But in the mornings and evenings, when the light is soft, the greens, reds, oranges, and purples really come to life.

In addition to the main drive, which provides numerous places to pull off, sit, and enjoy the fascinating landscape, the park has many hiking trails out into the moonscape. Park rangers offer many interesting programs on the park's geology and animal life, as well as occasional stargazing tours. Because there are few buildings in the area, there is no light pollution, so the night sky is spectacular, with its fantastic view of millions of stars. An evening in the near-absolute darkness of the Badlands is not to be missed.

The Badlands Loop Scenic Byway weaves in and out among the park's canyons, cliffs, and prairie.

The southern part of the park, which is much less visited than its northern counterpart, is actually in the Pine Ridge Indian Reservation. The reservation itself offers a heart-wrenching departure from the prepackaged tourism of much of South Dakota. Driving south into Pine Ridge, you enter Shannon County, the poorest county in the nation. The roads become rougher, filled with potholes. The ramshackle houses are few and far between. Every now and then you pass through a small town, which basically consists of a little store and a café. The dry and desolate landscape is a reminder that Indian reservations always ended up on the worst land, the land that was of no use to the white men.

Down the road from the town of Porcupine, near a junction not far from the town of Wounded Knee, is a historical marker that tells about the Wounded Knee Massacre. On a nearby hill stand a graveyard and a memorial to those who died at the battle. Up on that hill there is no noise but the sound of the relentless wind and an occasional passing car. Looking around from the solitude of the graveyard at the surrounding hills and valleys, it is easy to imagine the day, a little more than a hundred years ago, when the bleeding bodies of men, women, and children lay in the snow. There are no souvenir stands at Wounded Knee, no guided tours, no place to buy a hot dog or an ice cream cone. Its bleak sadness makes it the most moving site in all the state.

In Pine Ridge, the largest town on the reservation, there is another interesting site. The Heritage Center at Red Cloud Indian School has a fine collection of Native American art, including painting, sculpture, and traditional crafts such as beadwork and porcupine quillwork. Every year the center hosts an art show by Native American artists from all over the United States, the largest such show in the country.

FREE ICE WATER

There are a lot of tourist traps in South Dakota and a lot of billboards on the freeway from Sioux Falls to the Black Hills. But there is only one tourist trap that is famous because of its billboards—Wall Drug.

In 1931, Ted and Dorothy Hustead bought the drugstore in the tiny town of Wall, on the outskirts of the Badlands. This was long before air-conditioning, and one scorching South Dakota day, Dorothy realized that the tourists driving from the Badlands to the Black Hills were probably hot and thirsty. So the Husteads put up signs advertising free ice water at Wall Drug. Sure enough, the signs attracted plenty of new customers.

The signs multiplied along the roads leading to and from Wall, informing drivers exactly how many miles they were from Wall Drug. These signs became legend and turned up all over the world. From Italy to India to the Arctic Circle, no matter where you were you might suddenly find out how far it was to that small town in South Dakota.

Today Wall Drug has signs on freeways, on highways, and on byways. When you're past Wall Drug you'll see signs informing you that you missed it. There are more than three thousand Wall Drug signs all over the nation.

Wall Drug has taken over most of the town of Wall. It has become more of a mall than a drugstore, with forty little shops that sell everything from donuts to boots, and an awful lot of tacky souvenirs in between. On a hot summer day, 20,000 people pass through Wall Drug, looking for ice water.

TEN LARGEST CITIES

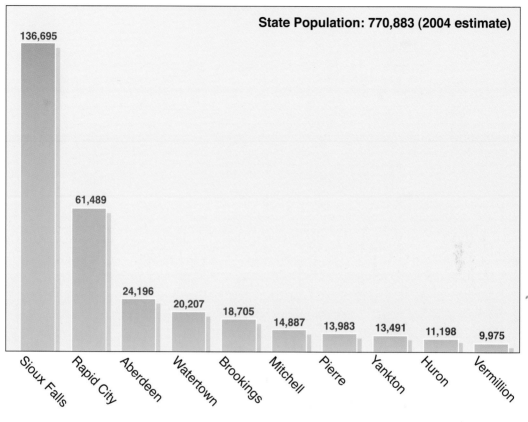

State Population: 770,883 (2004 estimate)

City	Population
Sioux Falls	136,695
Rapid City	61,489
Aberdeen	24,196
Watertown	20,207
Brookings	18,705
Mitchell	14,887
Pierre	13,983
Yankton	13,491
Huron	11,198
Vermillion	9,975

THE BLACK HILLS

To many tourists, a vacation in South Dakota means a trip to the Black Hills. The hills cover a relatively small area but are jam-packed with historical sites, fun activities, and natural beauty. Even the roads are tourist attractions. They were built to lure visitors with their magnificent vistas and scenery. The roads through the craggy hills are so winding (some even have the curving switch-backs of "pigtail" bridges) that driving is very slow going. The route of the most famous of these, the Iron Mountain Road, was laid out by Peter Nor-beck, a former South Dakota governor and senator who loved the Black Hills

A visit to the Black Hills wouldn't be complete without a drive along Iron Mountain Road.

more than anywhere else. When people objected to the road's roundabout route, Norbeck replied, "This is not a commercial highway, it's a scenic road. To do the scenery half-justice, people should drive twenty miles per hour or under; to do it full justice, they should get out and walk!"

Undoubtedly the most famous site in the Black Hills is Mount Rushmore. In the early 1920s, historian Doane Robinson had an idea. He thought it would be great to honor legendary western heroes such as Lewis and Clark, Buffalo Bill Cody, and Sioux warriors by carving a huge sculpture in the Black Hills. But after sculptor Gutzon Borglum took the job, he informed Robinson that his subjects would be national heroes, not western ones. So peering out placidly from the side of the mountain are Presidents George Washington, Thomas Jefferson, Theodore Roosevelt, and Abraham Lincoln.

Mount Rushmore sculptor Gutzon Borglum once said, "A monument's dimensions should be determined by the importance of the events commemorated."

Upon first seeing Mount Rushmore, many people are surprised by how small it looks. But don't be fooled. It's actually huge. George Washington's face is sixty feet tall. If the face had a body, the sculpture would be 465 feet tall.

Down the road a way, another mountain is being carved that dwarfs Mount Rushmore. This will eventually be a giant sculpture of Crazy Horse sitting on his steed and pointing into the distance. Crazy Horse was a great Lakota warrior who was never defeated in battle, was never photographed, and never wore white-men's clothes or accepted any other part of white culture. Work on the sculpture began in 1946. Crazy Horse's face, which is 87.5 feet tall, was finished in 1998. Also visible are much of the horse's head and Crazy Horse's outstretched arm. When completed, the sculpture will be more than 600 feet long and 563 feet tall, and carved so that you can look at it from all sides.

The Crazy Horse Memorial is carved by a crew who use "precision explosive engineering" to carve and shape the mountain.

The Black Hills are famous for their abundance of caves. The hills were formed when molten rock from deep inside the earth forced its way upward through a layer of limestone. This left cracks in the limestone. Water running through these cracks gradually wore away the rock and over millions of years created the vast cave mazes in the hills. The most famous is Wind Cave National Park. Wind Cave is renowned for its delicate formations, such as boxwork—a paper-thin formation that looks like a honeycomb, is easily broken, and is found in only one other cave in the world. Other beautiful formations that can be seen on

Popcorn and frostwork formations can be found in Wind Cave.

tours of Wind Cave are frostwork, which looks like a tiny bush covered with frost, and popcorn, which looks just like its name.

One of the biggest attractions in the Black Hills is the Mammoth Site. Mammoths were giant creatures that looked something like elephants; each of them ate seven hundred pounds of grass every day. About 26,000 years ago there was a pond where the site is now located. Mammoths went there for a dip, but the sides of the pond were too steep and slippery for them to get back out. Over time the watering hole disappeared, but the mammoth skeletons remained. In 1974, while the site was being leveled so that a house could be built there, a worker came across a glimmering white, seven-foot-long tusk.

The remains of dozens of mammoths can be seen at the Mammoth Site.

Work on the housing project stopped. As geologists began excavating the site, they found more and more bones. Rather than carting them all off to a museum or a laboratory, they decided to leave most of the bones and tusks where they lay and to remove just the dirt from around them. This means that when you visit the site, not only can you see the bones as they were found but you can also sometimes see paleontologists at work, carefully digging, sifting, and scratching the dirt. So far, they have uncovered the remains of more than fifty mammoths, making it the largest find of this kind anywhere in the world. And they are nowhere near the bottom of the hole yet.

Despite all these attractions, perhaps the greatest sight in the Black Hills are the hills themselves—their rocky peaks, dark forests, and clear streams—and the abundant wildlife. Driving through the hills, you will likely see white-tailed deer, pronghorns, mule deer, and prairie dogs. If you're lucky, you will see coyote and bighorn sheep. And you will most definitely see buffalo.

Both Wind Cave National Park and Custer State Park have herds of the magnificent creatures roaming free. You will see old buffalo and calves, males and females, grazing, rolling around on their backs, or just standing stock-still, seeming to stare at you. Some will be off in the distance, but many will be right outside the window of your car. It's virtually impossible to drive through these parks without seeing a buffalo. In fact, you will see so many that soon you will not even want to bother to stop and take a picture. Of course, when a herd of the giant beasts park themselves in the road without the least concern for your desire to get back to town for dinner, there's nothing to do but wait. In South Dakota, that's what passes for a traffic jam.

Bison roam freely in Custer State Park's 71,000 acres.

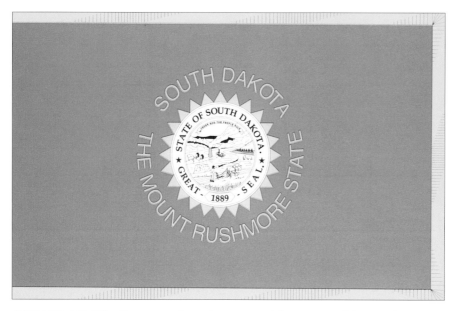

THE FLAG: *The flag was adopted in 1992. The state seal lies at the center and is encircled by a yellow sunburst against a blue background. The words "South Dakota The Mount Rushmore State" are printed around the sunburst.*

THE SEAL: *The border reads "State of South Dakota, Great Seal, 1889." The picture inside the circle shows the elements of the state's economy. A farmer plows in the foreground. A steamboat, a smelting furnace, and grazing cattle in the background represent trade, industry, and agriculture. The state motto, "Under God the People Rule," is written at the top of the picture.*

State Survey

Statehood: November 2, 1889

Origin of Name: South Dakota comes from the Sioux Indians who called themselves Dakota or Lakota, meaning "friends" or "allies."

Nicknames: The Mount Rushmore State, The Sunshine State, The Coyote State

Capital: Pierre

Motto: "Under God the People Rule"

Bird: Chinese ring-necked pheasant

Animal: Coyote

Fish: Walleye

Flower: American pasqueflower

Tree: Black Hills spruce

Mineral: Rose quartz

Gem: Fairburn agate

Insect: Honeybee

Musical instrument: Fiddle

Soil: Houdek

Grass: Western wheatgrass

Colors: Blue and gold

Coyote

Pasqueflower

"HAIL! SOUTH DAKOTA"

One hundred fifty-eight songs were submitted in a statewide contest for an official state song. The judges chose "Hail! South Dakota," composed by Deecort Hammitt, director of the Alcester municipal band. The song was officially adopted on March 5, 1943.

Words & Music by Deecort Hammitt

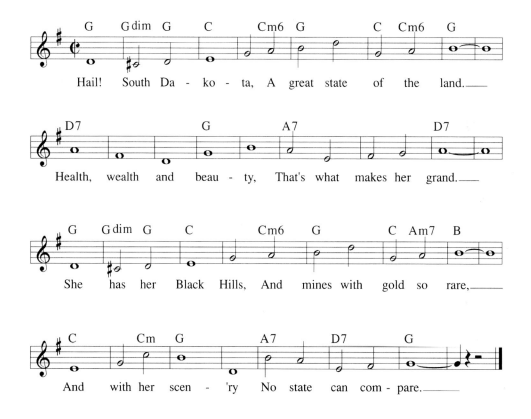

GEOGRAPHY

Highest Point: Harney Peak, 7,242 feet

Lowest Point: Big Stone Lake, 962 feet

Area: 77,122 square miles

Greatest Distance North to South: 237 miles

Greatest Distance East to West: 383 miles

Bordering States: Montana and Wyoming to the west, North Dakota to the north, Minnesota and Iowa to the east, Nebraska to the south

Hottest Recorded Temperature: 120 degrees Fahrenheit at Gann Valley on July 5, 1936

Coldest Recorded Temperature: −58 degrees Fahrenheit at McIntosh on February 17, 1936

Average Annual Precipitation: 18 inches

Major Rivers: Bad, Big Sioux, Cheyenne, Grand, James, Little Missouri, Missouri, Vermillion, White

Major Lakes: Francis Case, Oahe, Sharpe, Lewis and Clark

Trees: ash, cottonwood, juniper, oak, pine, spruce

Wild Plants: American pasqueflower, black-eyed Susan, cactus, forget-me-not, goldenrod, lady's slipper, larkspur, mariposa lily, sunflower, wild orange geranium

Animals: buffalo, bighorn sheep, coyote, elk, mule deer, pronghorn, Rocky Mountain goat, white-tailed deer

Birds: Hungarian partridge, prairie chicken, Chinese ring-necked pheasant, sage grouse, sharp-tailed grouse, wild turkey

Black-eyed Susan

Fish: bass, bluegill, catfish, crappie, northern pike, paddlefish, perch, sauger, sturgeon, trout (brook, brown, rainbow), walleye

Endangered and Threatened Animals: American burying beetle, bald eagle, banded killifish, black-footed ferret, blacknose shiner, Blanding's turtle, central mudminnow, Eskimo curlew, finescale dace, gray wolf, interior least tern, lined snake, pallid sturgeon, peregrine falcon, whooping crane, Topeka shiner, scaleshell, Higgins eye, piping plover

Endangered and Threatened Plants: none endangered; one threatened: western prairie fringed orchid

Prairie chicken

TIMELINE

AD **500** Mound Builders appear along Big Sioux River.

1600s Arikara tribe settle along Missouri River.

1682 René-Robert Cavelier, Sieur de La Salle, claimed for France all land drained by Mississippi River, including area that became South Dakota.

1743 François de La Vérendrye and Louis-Joseph de La Vérendrye become first white explorers to reach South Dakota region.

1750–1790 Sioux drive Arikara up Missouri River.

1780 Pierre Dorion is first European settler in South Dakota.

1803 United States acquires South Dakota as part of Louisiana Purchase.

1804–1806 Meriwether Lewis and William Clark travel through South Dakota on their trek to the Pacific Northwest.

1817 Joseph La Framboise establishes first permanent settlement in South Dakota.

1861 Congress creates Dakota Territory, consisting of present-day North and South Dakota and much of Montana and Wyoming.

1862 Homestead Act passed to encourage settlement of western lands.

1868 Fort Laramie Treaty ends Red Cloud's War, which began in 1866, and establishes Great Sioux Reservation, which includes the Black Hills and other land as far as western Wyoming.

1874 U.S. government violates Fort Laramie Treaty after General George Custer confirms reports of gold in Black Hills; gold rush and Indian uprisings begin.

1876 Custer and his troops are defeated at the Battle of Little Bighorn. The Sioux then lose a series of battles and sign an agreement giving up claims to the Black Hills.

1889 South Dakota becomes a state.

1890 Last major confrontation between U.S. Army and Indians takes place with massacre of hundreds of Sioux near Wounded Knee Creek on the Pine Ridge Indian Reservation. Pierre becomes state capital.

1927 Work on Mount Rushmore begins.

1930s Severe drought in South Dakota and the rest of the Great Plains causes economic hardship.

1944 Congress authorizes construction of four hydroelectric dams on Missouri River to provide electric power, flood control, and irrigation.

1960s United States places missile sites in state.

1972 Senator George McGovern nominated as Democratic presidential candidate.

1973 Native American group occupies the town of Wounded Knee for seventy-one days.

1980 U.S. Supreme Court orders state to pay South Dakota Indian nations for land seized in 1877.

1991–1994 United States removes missiles from state as part of international nuclear disarmament agreement.

1993 Flooding causes severe crop damage estimated at more than $725 million.

1994 Senator Tom Daschle becomes the leader of the Democrats in the U.S. Senate.

2000 For the first time, more South Dakotans live in urban areas than in rural areas.

Early 2000s South Dakota suffers long-term drought.

2003 Sixty-seven tornadoes occur in South Dakota on June 23, a record for a single day in one state.

ECONOMY

Agricultural Products: cattle, corn, hay, hogs, oats, rye, sorghum, soybeans, sunflowers, wheat

Hay bales

Manufactured Products: clothing, electric and electronic equipment, food products, glass products, machinery

Natural Resources: beryl, feldspar, gold, mica, ponderosa pine, portland cement, silver, uranium

Business and Trade: communication, electric power, transportation

CALENDAR OF CELEBRATIONS

Volksmarch During the first weekend of June, the top of Thunderhead Mountain is open to the public. Tourists can view up close the work in progress on the Crazy Horse Memorial, which honors Crazy Horse and all other Native Americans. It is still under construction, but when completed, it will be 563 feet high and 641 feet long, and it will be the largest sculpture in the world.

Fort Sisseton Historical Festival During the first weekend of June, Fort Sisseton State Park hosts this festival, which celebrates pioneer days. It includes cavalry and infantry drills, square dancing, melodrama, frontier crafts, a costume ball, a draft-horse pull, and a Dutch-oven bake-off.

Laura Ingalls Wilder Pageant For three weekends (last weekend of June and first two weekends of July), this event in De Smet celebrates through drama the life and times of the famed children's author. Visitors can also enjoy wagon rides and other entertainment and tour the site of the Ingalls homestead.

Fort Sisseton cavalry drill

Black Hills Passion Play Each week in Spearfish during June, July, and August professional actors and residents reenact a Passion Play (religious drama on the life of Christ) that dates back more than seven hundred years to Oberammergau, Germany, where monks performed the play during Easter week. You can also take a backstage tour of the amphitheater.

Black Hills Roundup Cowboy days live on at the roundup. Since 1918, residents and visitors in Belle Fourche have celebrated the Fourth of July with three days of parades and rodeo events, such as bucking contests and steer roping.

Gold Discovery Days For two days in late July, the town of Custer celebrates the discovery of gold in French Creek in the Black Hills in 1874. The event includes rodeos, Indian dances, and a street carnival. There is also a pageant reenacting the Custer expedition, the gold rush, Old West lifestyles, and the effects of U.S. expansion on the Indian population.

Days of '76 Every August, Deadwood reenacts its history as a gold-rush boom town that attracted thousands of gold seekers as well as gunfighters and gamblers such as Wild Bill Hickok, Calamity Jane, Doc Holliday, and Wyatt Earp. The town celebrates those wild days with a rodeo, a pageant, reenactments of historical events, and games. In addition there is a three-mile parade of ox teams, covered wagons, buggies, stagecoaches, and pack mules.

Black Hills Roundup

Steam Threshing Jamboree Steam powers this annual August event at Prairie Village, near Madison. You can watch as antique farm machinery, a train, and even a merry-go-round are fired up by steam engines. This celebration of days gone by also includes parades, arts and crafts displays, square dancing, tractor pulls, and threshing demonstrations.

Rosebud Sioux Tribal Fair and Powwow Late August brings native tribes together in Rosebud for traditional dances, arts and crafts exhibits, and a buffalo dinner. This powwow, and others held during the summer, keep alive the traditions of the Great Sioux Nation and introduce its culture to visitors.

Black Hills Sawdust Day In one of the largest logging events in the region, lumberjacks show off their skills by competing in tree felling, saw bucking, ax and chain throwing, and wood splitting. It is held in Spearfish on the Saturday after Labor Day.

Corn Palace Festival The Corn Palace was built in 1892 to encourage settlement and prove how productive the soil was. It is decorated inside and outside with thousands of bushels of corn, grain, and grasses. For a week at the end of September, the end of the harvest season, this renowned and historic "palace" brings in name performers and speakers.

STATE STARS

George Lee "Sparky" Anderson (1934–), former manager of the Cincinnati Reds and the Detroit Tigers baseball team, was the first manager to achieve one hundred wins in both the American and National leagues and to manage World Series winners in both leagues. He was born in Bridgewater.

George Lee "Sparky" Anderson

L. Frank Baum (1856–1919), author of *The Wonderful Wizard of Oz* and thirteen other Oz books, grew up in the Aberdeen area, and edited and published that city's weekly paper. He also wrote *Father Goose, His Book* and other children's books. He was born in Chittenango, New York.

Gutzon Borglum (1867–1941), the sculptor most famous for his gigantic work at Mount Rushmore, was born in Idaho. Borglum studied art in San Francisco and Paris, where he became friends with the French sculptor Auguste Rodin. He moved to New York in 1901 and became a popular sculptor of portraits and public monuments, including a six-ton marble head of Abraham Lincoln for the U.S. Capitol rotunda. He began work on Mount Rushmore in 1927. He and his crew spent twelve years,

Gutzon Borglum

using pneumatic drills and dynamite, to carve the likenesses of Presidents Washington, Jefferson, Lincoln, and Theodore Roosevelt. Each head is sixty feet high.

Tom Brokaw (1940–   ), born in Webster, hosted NBC's *Today Show* for six years. He became coanchor with Roger Mudd of *NBC Nightly News* in 1981 and its sole anchor in 1983. He retired in 2004. Brokaw was White House correspondent during the Watergate scandal and President Nixon's resignation.

Tom Brokaw

Martha Jane "Calamity Jane" Burke (1852?–1903), born in Missouri, was a frontierswoman, expert rider, and markswoman. She also became a star of Buffalo Bill's Wild West Show. She told stories about being a Pony Express rider and a scout for General Custer, but it is difficult to know what is fact and what is legend about her life. One legend says she got her nickname because she told men it would be their calamity if they offended her. Dressed in men's clothing, she was a familiar figure in Deadwood. She is buried next to Wild Bill Hickok in the town's Mount Moriah Cemetery.

Crazy Horse (1842?–1877), chief of the Oglala Sioux, a group within the Lakota, participated in Red Cloud's War (1866–1868). During the Sioux uprising of 1876–1877, he defeated General George Crook at Rosebud Creek in Montana, and eight days later he helped to defeat General George Custer at the Battle of Little Bighorn. Crazy Horse surrendered to federal troops in May 1877 but was killed several months later, allegedly while trying to escape.

Hallie Flanagan (1890–1969), theater organizer, teacher, and playwright, was born in Redfield. She coauthored *Can You Hear Their Voices?*, a play about Arkansas farmers, and headed the Federal Theater Project, which brought live theater to millions of Americans during the Depression in the 1930s.

Gall (1840?–1894), a Sioux warrior, fought along with Crazy Horse and Sitting Bull in the Battle of Little Bighorn, in which General George Custer was killed and his Seventh Cavalry defeated.

Calamity Jane

Hamlin Garland (1860–1940), a writer, was born in West Salem, Wisconsin; his family homestead was in Ordway, South Dakota. His books included *Main-Travelled Roads*, *Prairie Folks*, *Rose of Dutcher's Coolly*, *A Son of the Middle Border*, *The Book of the American Indian*, and *A Daughter of the Middle Border*, which won a Pulitzer Prize. Garland's works described the frustrations and hardships of pioneering on the Plains.

Alvin H. Hansen (1887–1975), an economist, was born in Viborg. He believed that an economic depression like that of the 1930s could be prevented by government planning, and he urged greater government spending on roads, hospitals, schools, and housing.

Mary Hart (1950–   ), born in Sioux Falls, is a television talk-show host best known for her work on *Entertainment Tonight*.

James Butler "Wild Bill" Hickok (1837–1876), was a legendary Indian fighter and frontier marshal. Born in Illinois, he left his family's farm when he was eighteen and traveled west to the Nebraska Territory. He was a federal scout during the Civil War and later toured with Buffalo Bill's Wild West Show. During the gold rush of 1876 he moved to Deadwood, where he was killed in a saloon and buried in the town's cemetery, along with other legends of the Wild West, including Calamity Jane.

Mary Hart

Hubert Horatio Humphrey Jr. (1911–1978), was born in Wallace and served as the thirty-eighth vice president of the United States (1965–1969). Humphrey worked as a pharmacist before becoming involved in Minnesota politics. He was elected mayor of Minneapolis in 1945 and U.S. senator in 1948. He served in the Senate until 1964, when he was chosen as President Lyndon Johnson's running mate. He ran for president in 1968 and was narrowly defeated by Richard Nixon. He returned to the Senate in 1971 and unsuccessfully sought the Democratic presidential nomination in 1972 and 1976. Humphrey was a strong supporter of civil rights.

Hubert Humphrey Jr.

Oscar Howe (1915–1983), an artist and a Dakota Indian of the Yanktonai tribe, was born in Crow Creek. His abstract paintings and murals, displayed throughout the state, depict Native American life and spirituality. He taught at the University of South Dakota, and in 1960, he was named the state's artist laureate.

Ernest O. Lawrence (1901–1958), 1939 Nobel Prize winner in physics, was born in Canton. His invention the cyclotron, sometimes called an atom smasher, which accelerates atomic particles to produce artificial radioactivity, has been important in the fields of nuclear physics and medicine. The element lawrencium is named for him. He was also instrumental in the development of the atomic bomb.

Ernest O. Lawrence

George McGovern (1922–), South Dakota's senator for three terms, was born in Avon. He was the Democratic nominee for the U.S. presidency in 1972. He was overwhelmingly defeated by Richard Nixon despite strong support from opponents of the Vietnam War. First elected to the Senate in 1962, he had worked as a professor of history, a U.S. representative, and a director of the Food for Peace program. He lost his bid for a fourth Senate term in 1980.

George McGovern

Allen Neuharth (1924–), born in Eureka, founded the newspaper *USA Today* in 1982. He was formerly chairman of Gannett Company, which owns a chain of newspapers.

Red Cloud (1822–1909), born in Nebraska, was head chief of the Oglala Sioux, a group within the Lakota. He led the Indians in the conflict with the U.S. Army that became known as Red Cloud's War (1866–1868). This war ended with Red Cloud's signing of the Fort Laramie Treaty in 1868. He went to live on a reservation, losing his status as head chief in 1881.

Ole E. Rolvaag (1876–1931) is best known for his realistic writings about Norwegian settlers on the Dakota prairies. Born in Norway, he immigrated to the United States in 1896 and became a citizen in 1908. Two novels that he wrote in his native language were translated into English and combined as *Giants in the Earth*.

Earl Sande (1898–1968) won horse racing's Triple Crown in 1930 riding Gallant Fox. Born in Groton, he was a well-accomplished jockey, winning more than 950 races, including the Kentucky Derby three times and the Belmont Stakes five times. He was named to the Racing Hall of Fame in 1955.

Sitting Bull (1831–1890) was a great Sioux leader of the Hunkpapa Lakota nation. Born on the Grand River, he opposed the surrender of land and mining rights to the United States after gold was discovered in the Black Hills. He fought along with Gall and Crazy Horse at the Battle of Little Bighorn, then fled to Canada. He returned in 1881 and was imprisoned for two years, then traveled with Buffalo Bill's Wild West Show. Sitting Bull again became active in Indian affairs, for which he was arrested in 1890. He was killed by tribal police during the disturbance following his arrest.

Joseph Ward (1838–1889) was a leader in South Dakota's efforts to become a state and is credited with establishing its public-education system. In 1872 he founded Yankton Academy, which became the first college in the upper Mississippi River valley. Ward was born in New York State.

Sitting Bull

Laura Ingalls Wilder (1867–1957), born in Wisconsin, lived in De Smet and wrote about growing up on the frontier. Her books included *Little House on the Prairie*, *On the Banks of Plum Creek*, *By the Shores of Silver Lake*, *The Long Winter*, and *Little Town on the Prairie*.

Korczak Ziolkowski (1908–1982), a Polish orphan who grew up in Boston, was the sculptor behind the still-unfinished Crazy Horse Memorial, which when finished will be the largest sculpture in the

Laura Ingalls Wilder

world—563 feet tall and 641 feet long. After he died, his family continued his work.

TOUR THE STATE

Badlands National Park (near Rapid City) This "moonscape" of canyons, spires, and razor-edged ridges became a national monument in 1939 and a national park in 1978. You can see bison, pronghorns, mule deer, prairie dogs, and Rocky Mountain bighorn sheep and learn about the wildlife and geology from exhibits, lectures, and other events led by park rangers.

Mammoth Site (Hot Springs) Visit the largest concentration of mammoth bones found in the Western Hemisphere. Take a guided tour of current diggings, learn the history of the site, and view the remains of mammoths, giant short-faced bears, and other animals that died there more than 25,000 years ago.

Rapid City Dinosaur Park (Rapid City) Visitors can see life-size steel-and-cement models of dinosaurs that once roamed the land that is now South Dakota.

Rapid City Dinosaur Park

Journey Museum (Rapid City) The Sioux Indian Museum and Crafts Center (exhibits of historic and contemporary Native American crafts) and the Minnilusa Pioneer Museum (exhibits of historical items from pioneer days in the Dakotas) are both here.

Thunderhead Underground Falls (Rapid City) This is one of the oldest (1878) gold-mine tunnels in the Black Hills. The underground falls are an easy six-hundred-foot walk from the entrance.

Jewel Cave National Monument (near Custer) With more than 133 miles of passageways, this is the third-longest cave system in the world. Take a scenic or historic tour of the monument. If you are older than sixteen years and in good condition, you can try spelunking (exploring caves).

Wind Cave National Park (near Custer) The park, established in 1903, is really two parks—one below ground and one at the surface. The park is named for the strong currents that blow in and out of the cave entrance. There are more than forty-four miles of underground passages in the park, connecting chambers with names such as Garden of Eden and Blue Grotto. You have a choice of guided tours of various lengths. Above ground are grasslands, forests, and a wildlife preserve. You can also tour the surrounding Black Hills.

Crazy Horse Memorial (near Custer) This giant sculpture of the great Sioux chief is being carved out of a granite mountain. Sculptor Korczak Ziolkowski worked on it from 1948 until his death in 1982, and members of his family have continued the work. At the base, you can see scale models of the sculpture and exhibits that explain the drilling and blasting process. The Indian Museum of North America is also here.

Crazy Horse Memorial

Custer State Park (near Hot Springs) One of the world's largest herds of bison roam this 73,000-acre state park. As you drive around the eighteen-mile Wildlife Loop, watch for the bison as well as mountain goats, Rocky Mountain bighorn sheep, burros, and other creatures. Visitors can fish, swim, ride horses, rent paddleboats, bike, and camp.

1880 Train (Hill City) Ride along tracks built during the gold rush on the Black Hills Central Railroad train pulled by a steam engine. The two-hour round trip between Hill City and Keystone takes you through scenic national forests and meadows.

Mount Rushmore National Memorial (Keystone) The heads of Presidents Washington, Jefferson, Lincoln, and Theodore Roosevelt are carved on the face of the mountain. Sculptor Gutzon Borglum had intended to sculpt them to the waist, but he died before completing the work. An orientation center provides information about the memorial, and the sculptor's studio features tools, models, paintings, and photographs of the construction process.

National Museum of Woodcarving (Custer) Thousands of woodcarvings are displayed, including works by one of the original Disney animators, who created miniature and life-size figures that move and speak.

Mount Rushmore National Memorial

Mount Moriah Cemetery (Deadwood) You'll see the Wild West of legend when you visit the town of Deadwood. Take a tour of the town and visit Mount Moriah Cemetery, commonly known as Boot Hill, where legendary figures from the gold rush days are buried.

The Ghosts of Deadwood Gulch Wax Museum (Deadwood) This museum features more than seventy life-size wax figures depicting life in the area, from the arrival of the first white people through the Wild West days, when Calamity Jane, Deadwood Dick, Wild Bill Hickok, and other colorful characters gathered here to cash in on the gold rush.

Black Hills Mining Museum (Lead) Exhibits, videos, photographs, and life-size figures take you back through the development of a mine that has been in operation since 1876. A tour of a simulated mine helps you understand how a gold mine operates. You can even try panning for gold yourself.

Homestake Gold Mine Surface Tours (Lead) Homestake Gold Mine was one of the oldest and largest gold mines in the Western Hemisphere. Take a one-hour surface tour of its operation. If you've ever wondered how gold is extracted from the earth, watch an audiovisual presentation about the mining and refining of this valuable substance.

Fort Sisseton State Park (Lake City) Fourteen of the fort's brick and stone buildings, built in 1864 as part of the U.S. Army's frontier post, have been restored. You can also visit other historical exhibits.

Laura Ingalls Wilder Memorial (De Smet) If you are a fan of the Little House books, you won't want to miss this memorial to the author. It includes the family home from 1879, a replica of a schoolhouse, and other buildings mentioned in her books.

Prairie Village (Madison) Get a feel for pioneer life by spending time at this replica of a pioneer town. It includes forty restored buildings, including a one-room schoolhouse, theater, cabins, and churches, as well as antique farm equipment, a steam merry-go-round, and steam trains.

National Music Museum (Vermillion) Music lovers will want to see this collection of more than three thousand musical instruments. The exhibit of Italian stringed instruments from the sixteenth through eighteenth centuries features a Stradivari violin and a rare Stradivari guitar. Other collections include traditional instruments from the America's and around the world.

Dakota Territorial Museum (Yankton) This museum of pioneer life includes the restored Dakota Territorial Council Building and replicas of a railroad depot, a caboose, a rural schoolhouse, a dentist's office, a general store, a saloon, and a blacksmith shop.

Middle Border Museum and Oscar Howe Art Center (Mitchell) Works by Sioux artist Oscar Howe are exhibited here, along with other exhibits of Native American art and culture.

The Corn Palace (Mitchell) This fantastical building is decorated inside and outside with murals made from corn, other grains, and grasses.

The Corn Palace

Each year two thousand to three thousand bushels of various grains and grasses are used. Decorative panels inside were designed by artist Oscar Howe.

Enchanted World Doll Museum (Mitchell) More than four thousand dolls are housed in this castlelike museum complete with a moat, a drawbridge, and stained-glass windows. The dolls are arranged in four hundred scenes from fairy tales, nursery rhymes, children's books, and eighteenth- and nineteenth-century history.

Wounded Knee Historical Site (Pine Ridge) A monument marks the mass grave where two hundred Sioux men, women, and children were shot by the U.S. Army.

FUN FACTS

The geographic center of the United States, not including Alaska and Hawaii, is in western South Dakota, about seventeen miles west of Castle Rock.

The town of Sturgis was once a bullwhackers' (wagon drivers') stop on the way to Fort Meade. It was known as Scooptown because soldiers were "scooped"—cleaned out of all their money—by the cigar-smoking Poker Alice and other gamblers.

Want to predict the weather? Wind Cave can be your barometer. When the wind blows out of the cave, it means the barometer is falling. When the wind blows into the cave, the barometer is rising.

The Indian name for the Black Hills is *Paha Sapa*—"Hills of Black." Those hills are not really hills; they are domed mountains. And they are not really black—they are dense with dark-green trees. The *Paha Sapa* are older than the Rockies, the Alps, or the Himalayas.

Find Out More

If you'd like to find out more about South Dakota, look in your library, bookstore, or video store. Here are some titles to ask for:

STATE BOOKS

Hirschmann, Kris. *South Dakota: The Mount Rushmore State.* Milwaukee, WI: Gareth Stevens Publishing, 2003.

Sheperd, Donna Walsh. *South Dakota* (American the Beautiful series). Danbury, CT: Children's Press, 2001.

Yacowitz, Caryn. *South Dakota* (Sea to Shining Sea series). Danbury, CT: Children's Press, 2003.

SPECIAL INTEREST BOOKS

Kimmel, Elizabeth Cody. *As Far as the Eye Can Reach: Lewis and Clark's Westward Quest.* New York: Random House, 2003.

Patent, Dorothy Hinshaw. *Animals on the Trail with Lewis and Clark.* New York: Clarion, 2002.

Robbins, Ken. *Thunder on the Plains: The Story of the American Buffalo.* New York: Atheneum, 2001.

Waldman, Neil. *Wounded Knee.* New York: Atheneum, 2001.

WEB SITES

State of South Dakota

www.state.sd.us/

For news, history, facts, statistics, and much, much more.

Argus Leader

www.argusleader.com/

Read this Sioux Falls newspaper to keep up with what's happening in South Dakota.

Just For Kids

www.state.sd.us/governor/Main/kids/kl.htm

This Web page includes many links to kid-friendly Web sites and games on South Dakota.

South Dakota

www.kidskonnect.com/

Fun facts about South Dakota plus links to the important sites in the state.

South Dakota State Parks

www.sdgfp.info/parks/

This Web site is the place to come for information on South Dakota's state parks.

Index

Page numbers in **boldface** are illustrations and charts.

ABOUT THE AUTHOR

Melissa McDaniel is the author of more than twenty books for young people on subjects ranging from the movies to the ocean floor. She particularly enjoys writing about interesting places because it gives her a chance to travel and learn more about the world. When not exploring the country, Melissa lives in New York City with her husband, Martin, and her daughter, Iris.